From the Other Side of Night
Del otro lado de la noche

CAMINO DEL SOL
A Latina and Latino Literary Series

From the Other Side of Night
Del otro lado de la noche

NEW AND SELECTED POEMS

Francisco X. Alarcón

With a selection of translations by
Francisco Aragón

The University of Arizona Press   Tucson

The University of Arizona Press
© 2002 Francisco X. Alarcón
All rights reserved
♾ This book is printed on acid-free, archival-quality paper.
Manufactured in the United States of America

07 06 05 04 03   6 5 4 3 2

Library of Congress Cataloging-in-Publication Data

Alarcón, Francisco X., 1954-
   From the other side of night–Del otro lado de la noche : new and
selected poems / Francisco X. Alarcón ; with a selection of
translations by Francisco Aragón.
      p. cm.
ISBN 0-8165-2180-8 (pbk. : alk. paper)
1. Mexico—Poetry. 2. Mexican Americans—Poetry.
3. Indians of North America—Poetry. I. Aragón, Francisco.
II. Title.
   PS3551.L22 F77 2002
   811'.54—dc21   2001004398

British Library Cataloguing-in-Publication Data
A catalogue record for this book is available from the
British Library.

Publication of this book is made possible in part by the
proceeds of a permanent endowment created with the
assistance of a Challenge Grant from the National
Endowment for the Humanities, a federal agency.

To all in our *familia*
in blood, in spirit, in life—
and to all those willing to turn
nights into days for others

En una noche oscura
con ansias en amores inflamada,
¡oh dichosa ventura!
salí sin ser notada,
estando ya mi casa sosegada ...

En la noche dichosa
en secreto, que nadie me veía,
ni yo miraba cosa,
sin otra luz y guía,
sino la que en el corazón ardía ...

—San Juan de la Cruz (1542–1591), *Noche oscura*

Contents

Acknowledgments

Poems from the last section of this collection, "From the Other Side of Night / Del otro lado de la noche," were previously published in the following periodicals, journals, and books: "Para nosotros / For Us," "Encuentro / Encounter," and "Del otro lado de la noche / From the Other Side of Night," *La Jornada Semanal* (Mexico City), Sunday, May 27, 2001; "Boricua," *El Andar* (Santa Cruz, Calif.,) summer 2000; "Para nosotros / For Us" and "Pro vida / For Life," in *Chicano/Latino Homoerotic Identities,* edited by David William Foster, Garland Reference Library of the Humanities, vol. 2117, Latin American Studies, vol. 16 (New York and London: Garland Publishing, 1999); "Blues del SIDA / AIDS Blues," in *The Geography of Home: California's Poetry of Place,* selected and edited by Christopher Buckley and Gary Young (Berkeley, Calif.: Heyday Books, 1999); "Encuentro," in *Los vasos comunicantes: antología de poesía chicana,* edited by Jaime B. Rosa (Murcia, Spain: Huerga y Fierro Editores, 1999); "Tlazoltéotl," in *Goddess of the Americas / La Diosa de las Américas: Writings on the Virgen of Guadalupe,* edited by Ana Castillo (New York: Riverhead Books, 1996). *Sonnets to Madness and Other Misfortunes,* by Francisco X. Alarcón, copyright © 2001 by Francisco X. Alarcón, was reprinted by permission of Creative Arts Book Company, Berkeley, California.

Tattoos

Tattoos

poems
fill up
pages

tattoos
puncture
flesh

Raíces

mis raíces
las cargo
siempre
conmigo
enrolladas
me sirven
de almohada

Roots

I carry
my roots
with me
all the time
rolled up
I use them
as my pillow

Dialéctica del amor

para el mundo
no somos nada
pero aquí juntos
—tú y yo—
somos el mundo

Dialectics of Love

to the world
we are nothing
but here together
—you and I—
are the world

Eros

no hay
llave
para tu
puerta

sólo
lengua
para tu
cerradura

Eros

there is
no key
for your
door

only
a tongue
for your
keyhole

Banderas	Flags
trapos	stupid
imbéciles	rags
empapados	soaked
en sangre	in blood

Oración

quiero un dios
de cómplice
que se trasnoche
en tugurios
de mala fama
y los sábados
se levante tarde

un dios
que chifle
por las calles
y tiemble
ante los labios
de su amor

un dios
que haga cola
a la entrada
de los cines
y tome café
con leche

un dios
que escupa
sangre de
tuberculoso
y no tenga ni
para el camión

un dios
que se desmaye

Prayer

I want a god
as my accomplice
who spends nights
in houses
of ill repute
and gets up late
on Saturdays

a god
who whistles
through the streets
and trembles
before the lips
of his lover

a god
who waits in line
at the entrance
of movie houses
and likes to drink
café au lait

a god
who spits
blood from
tuberculosis and
doesn't even have
enough for bus fare

a god
knocked

de un macanazo
de policía
en un mitin
de protesta

un dios
que se orine
de miedo ante
el resplandor
de los electrodos
de tortura

un dios
que le punce
hasta el último
hueso
y muerda el aire
de dolor

un dios desempleado
un dios en huelga
un dios hambriento
un dios fugitivo
un dios en exilio
un dios encabronado

un dios
que anhele
desde la cárcel
un cambio
en el orden
de las cosas

quiero
un dios
más dios

unconscious
by the billy club
of a policeman
at a demonstration

a god
who pisses
out of fear
before the flaring
electrodes
of torture

a god
who hurts
to the last
bone and
bites the air
in pain

a jobless god
a striking god
a hungry god
a fugitive god
an exiled god
an enraged god

a god
who longs
from jail
for a change
in the order
of things

I want a
more godlike
god

I Used to Be Much Much Darker

I used to be
much much darker
dark as la tierra
recién llovida
and dark was all
I ever wanted—
dark tropical
mountains
dark daring
eyes
dark tender lips
and I would sing
dark
dream dark
talk only dark

happiness
was to spend
whole
afternoons
tirado como foca
bajo el sol
"you're already
so dark
muy prieto
too indio!"
some would lash
at my happy
darkness but
I could only
smile back

now I'm not as
dark as I once was
quizás sean
los años
maybe I'm too
far up north
not enough sun
not enough time
but anyway
up here "dark"
is only for
the ashes—
the stuff
lonely nights
are made of

Un Beso Is Not a Kiss

un beso
es una puerta
que se abre
un secreto
compartido
un misterio
con alas

un beso
no admite
testigos
un beso can't
be captured
traded
or sated

un beso
is not just
a kiss —
un beso is
more dangerous
sometimes
even fatal

Ya vas, carnal

Oscura luz

teñida de noche
tengo la piel
en este país
de mediodía

pero más oscura
tengo el alma
de tanta luz
que llevo adentro

Dark Light

my skin is dark
as the night
in this country
of noontime

but my soul
is even darker
from all the light
I carry inside

Prófugo	Fugitive
he tenido	I've had
que soportar	to bear
los días	the days
anónimo	anonymously
como sombra	like a shadow
escurrirme	slip
por la ciudad	through the city
sin causar	without raising
sospecha	suspicions
he rodeado	I've avoided
innumerables	countless
caminos	roads
saltado	jumped
cada cerca	every fence
huyendo	always
siempre	fleeing
con una prisa	with a haste
que me muerde	that bites
los talones	my heels
y apenas	and barely
me deja	lets me
respirar	breathe
ocultándome	hiding behind
tras tantas	so many
quimeras	illusions
durante	for so
tantos años	many years
que ahora	that now
ya ni distingo	I don't

el rostro
de mi alma
ni recuerdo
qué me llevó
a esta vida
de prófugo

mi crimen
debe haber
sido enorme
como
la oscuridad
que acarrea
mi pena

ante todo
he procurado
la compañía
muda
de la noche

he aprendido
a disimular
casi todo
pero
todavía
me delata
junto a ti
el desbocado
palpitar
de mi corazón

even know
the face
of my soul
or recall
what brought me
to this fugitive's life

my crime
must have
been
as huge as
the darkness
found in
my punishment

above all
I've sought
the mute
company
of night

I've learned
to fake
nearly everything
but
still
when next to you
I'm given away
by the empty
pounding
of my heart

Canto a las tortillas

yo sigo
nombrando *Nana*
a la Tierra

alimentándome
del canto
sembrado

por los antiguos
en las más humildes
tortillas de la vida

In Praise of Tortillas

I go on
calling *Nana*
to the Earth

feeding on
the canto
sown

by the ancient ones
inside the humblest
tortillas of life

Acusado de todo

estoy de pie
quieto
lejos muy lejos
en mi celda

sin palabras
con mi vida
hecha nudo
en la garganta

sin más delito
que mi pobreza
y estas ansias
locas de vivir

acusado de todo
nada me queda
sino sacarle
filo al alma

Patria
en Aztlán

nosotros
los extranjeros
en tierra propia
los que
regalamos
todo lo que
todavía
no nos roban

los reducidos
a sombras
los que
llevamos
en los ojos
una noche
cruel
y oscura

sólo nos
reconocemos
en las estrellas:
sabemos
que nuestra
patria está
por hacerse

Patria
in Aztlán

foreigners
in our own
native land
giving away
everything
they haven't
yet stolen
from us

reduced
to shadows
carrying
inside
our eyes
a dark
and cruel
night

we only
recognize
ourselves
in the stars —
we know
our country
has yet to be built!

Zenthroamérika

nadie tiene
nada que decir
frente a tanto
dolor

nadie ni nada
ante este río
de muerte
atroz

este pulsar
congelado
en párpados
torturados

dedos sin uñas
sílabas rotas
y la historia
muda

A Shadow's Fate

tough
being a shadow
always trailing
someone else's
footsteps
not being able
to scream
or cry out
when suddenly
stamped on

what
a faceless fate
being sprawled
in oblivion
in the middle
of the day
speechless
on a dirty
downtown
sidewalk

a shadow
always
attached to
someone else's
life without
the freedom
to choose
whom
to follow
and love

Bienaventurados	Blessed
los que dejan	those who toss
su cruz	their crosses
y se atreven	and dare
a vivir	to live out
de ternura	their tenderness
los que unen	those who bring
cuerpo	together body
alma	soul
y mundo	and world
en un beso	in a kiss
los exiliados	blessed
del amor	the exiles
los raros	of love
de espíritu	the queer
bienaventurados	in spirit
porque llevan	for they carry
enterrada	deep inside
¡la semilla	the seed
de la verdadera	of true
liberación!	liberation!

Puente

extiende
los brazos
extiéndelos
que toquen
tus manos
mi orilla

yo recorreré
tu cuerpo
como quien
cruza
un puente
y se salva

Bridge

extend
your arms
extend them
until your hands
touch the edge
of my body

I will travel
across your body
like someone
who crosses
a bridge
and saves himself

Body in Flames / Cuerpo en llamas

English translations by Francisco Aragón

Poeta encarcelado

cada mañana
me despierto
solo
fingiendo

que mi brazo
es la carne
de tu cuerpo
sobre mis labios

Imprisoned Poet

every morning
I awaken
alone
pretending

that my arm
is your body's
flesh
on my lips

Tan real

todo ha sido
tan real:
las sillas
las puertas
tan sillas
tan puertas

ni un solo día
se ha saltado
el sol:
las noches
han seguido
a los días
y los días
a las noches
tan días
tan noches

todo
tan real y
tan cierto
como mis manos
tus manos
tus labios
y los míos
tan carne
tan sangre

todo
tan realmente cierto
y tan ciertamente real

So Real

everything
has been so real—
the chairs
the doors
so chairlike
so doorlike

the sun
has not skipped
a single day—
nights
have come
after days
and days
after nights
so daylike
so nightlike

everything
so real and
so certain
like my hands
your hands
your lips
and mine
so fleshlike
so bloodlike

everything
so really certain
and so certainly real

todo	everything
aun esta voz	even this voice
que a veces	that sometimes
se sabe	deep inside
en el fondo	feels itself
tan incierta	so uncertain
tan irreal	so unreal

Antigua canción	Old Song
todos llevamos	each of us carries
en el pecho	in our chest
una canción	a song
tan antigua	so old
que no sabemos	we don't know
si la aprendimos	if we learned it
cualquier noche	some night
entre el rumor	between the murmurs
de besos caídos	of fallen kisses
nuestros labios	our lips
nos sorprenden	surprise us
al entonar	when we voice
esta canción	this song
que es canto y	that is singing
llanto a la vez	and crying at once

En un barrio de Los Ángeles	In a Neighborhood in Los Angeles
el español	I learned
lo aprendí	Spanish
de mi abuela	from my grandma
mijito	*mijito*
no llores	don't cry
me decía	she'd tell me
en las mañanas	on the mornings
cuando salían	my parents
mis padres	would leave
a trabajar	to work
en las canerías	at the fish
de pescado	canneries
mi abuela	my grandma
platicaba	would chat
con las sillas	with chairs
les cantaba	sing them
canciones	old
antiguas	songs
les bailaba	dance
valses en	waltzes with them
la cocina	in the kitchen
cuando decía	when she'd say
niño barrigón	*niño barrigón*
se reía	she'd laugh

con mi abuela
aprendí
a contar nubes

a reconocer
en las macetas
la yerbabuena

mi abuela
llevaba lunas
en el vestido

la montaña
el desierto
el mar de México

en sus ojos
yo los veía
en sus trenzas

yo los tocaba
con su voz
yo los olía

un día
me dijeron:
se fue muy lejos

pero yo aún
la siento
conmigo

diciéndome
quedito al oído:
mijito

with my grandma
I learned
to count clouds

to recognize
mint leaves
in flowerpots

my grandma
wore moons
on her dress

Mexico's mountains
deserts
ocean

in her eyes
I'd see them
in her braids

I'd touch them
in her voice
smell them

one day
I was told:
she went far away

but still
I feel her
with me

whispering
in my ear:
mijito

Consejos de una madre	Advice of a Mother
hijo	*hijo*
ya cruzas	you've
los 33 años	turned 33
y no veo	yet I see
asientes	you heading
cabeza	nowhere
mira	look at
tu mundo	the world
alrededor	around you
tus primos	your cousins
están todos	are all
bien parados	standing firm
con los pies	their feet
plantados	planted on
en la tierra	the ground
mientras tú	while you
me duele	it hurts to see
verte así	you this way
gastando	wasting
tus ojos	your eyes
y tu tiempo	and your time
en eso	with those things
que llamas	you call
poemas	poems

Cuarto oscuro	Dark Room
en cada casa	in every house
hay un cuarto	there is a dark
oscuro	room
enclaustrado	hidden
entre paredes	by the walls
de otros cuartos	of other rooms
a los hombres	it doesn't seem
nos les parece	to bother
molestar	men
lo consideran	they consider it
lo más normal	the most normal
de la vida	thing in life
pero viven ahí	but there inside
en esa mazmorra	that cell without
sin ventanas	windows live
la madre	the mother
la hija	the daughter
la esposa	the wife

Mi padre

My Father

mi padre
y yo nos
saludamos

my father
and I greet
each other

cautelosos
como si
selláramos

guarded
as if
sealing

una tregua
en un campo
de batalla

a truce
on a
battlefield

nos sentamos
a comer como
dos extraños

we sit down
to eat like
two strangers

yo sé que
en el fondo
él también

yet I know
beneath it all
he too

rechaza
ese mal
esa locura

rejects
that affliction
that folly

esa pesadilla
llamada
macho

that nightmare
called
macho

Una pequeña
gran victoria

esa noche de verano
mi hermana dijo
     no
ya nunca más
se iba ella a poner
a lavar los trastes

mi madre sólo
se le quedó viendo
quizás deseando
haberle dicho
lo mismo
a su propia madre

ella también había odiado
sus tareas de "mujer"
de cocinar limpiar
siempre estar al tanto
de sus seis hermanos
y su padre

un pequeño trueno
sacudió la cocina
cuando silenciosos
nosotros recorrimos
con los ojos la mesa
de cinco hermanos

A Small but
Fateful Victory

that summer night
my sister said
     no
she was not going
to do the dishes
anymore

my mother only
stared at her
maybe wishing
she had said
the same thing
to her own mother

she too had hated
her "woman" chores
of cooking cleaning
always looking after
her six brothers
and her father

a small thunderclap
shook the kitchen
while us five
brothers quietly
exchanged looks
around the table

el repentino aprieto
se deshizo cuando
mi padre se puso
un mandil y abrió
la llave de agua
caliente en el fregadero

yo casi podía oír
la dulce música
de la victoria
                resonando
en los oídos de mi hermana
en la sonrisa de mi madre

the sudden impasse
was broken when
my father put on
an apron and started
to run the hot
water in the sink

I could almost hear
the sweet music
of victory
                ringing
in my sister's ears
in my mother's smile

Naturaleza criminal	Natural Criminal
soy	I am
un nómada	a nomad
en un país	in a country
de sedentarios	of settlers
una gota	a drop
de aceite	of oil
en un vaso	in a glass
de agua	of water
un nopal	a cactus
que florece	flowering
en donde	where one
no se puede	can't and
ni se debe	shouldn't
florecer	flourish
soy	I am
una herida	history's
todavía viva	fresh and
de la historia	living wound
mi crimen	my crime
ha sido ser	has been being
lo que he sido	what I've been
toda mi vida	all my life

El otro día me encontré a García Lorca

lo reconocí
por el moño
los labios
los ojos
olivos

lloraban
guitarras
y bailaba
flamenco
la tarde

de pronto
se paró
vino
directo
a mi mesa

y me plantó
un beso
como sol
andaluz
en la boca

The Other Day I Ran into García Lorca

I recognized him
by the slim bow tie
his lips
his eyes
olive colored

guitars
wept and
the afternoon
danced
flamenco

suddenly
he stood
walked
directly
to my table

and planted
a kiss like
an Andalusian
sun
on my lips

Todo es un
cuerpo inmenso

todo es
un cuerpo
inmenso

las sierras
muslos
extendidos

los árboles
en el valle
pelo en pecho

las bahías
bocas
lengua el mar

Everything Is an
Immense Body

everything is
an immense
body

the sierras
extended
thighs

the trees
in the valley
hair on a chest

the bays
mouths
tongue the sea

Anatomía presagiosa	Prophetic Anatomy
qué noches	what sort of nights
guardan callados	do your arms gather
tus brazos	in silence
qué auroras	what sort of dawns
prometen tiernos	do your lips
tus labios	tenderly promise
qué brisas	what sort of breezes
cargan gustosos	do your shoulders carry
tus hombros	without complaint
qué tempestades	what sort of storms
avecinan sin saberlo	does your hair
tus cabellos	unknowingly predict
qué hogueras	what sort of fires
qué precipicios	what sort of cliffs
qué heridas	what sort of wounds
anuncian	are announced
acaso proféticos	by your possibly
tus ojos	prophetic eyes

Cuerpo en llamas	Body in Flames
quiero dejar	I want to abandon
las palabras	words
ir y despertar	go and awaken
los sentidos	the senses
no quiero	I want
la memoria	no memory
sino abrazar	rather to embrace
cada instante	every instant
hasta la locura	to a frenzy
quiero pensar	I want to think
con los pies	with my feet
quiero llorar	I want to cry
con los hombros	with my shoulders
quiero prender	I want to set
fuego al cuerpo	my body on fire

Las flores son nuestras armas

we opened
the doors
of our homes

to greet them
they came in
and evicted us

we showed them
the open green
of our valleys

the sacred
blue
of the sky

they cut down
the trees
for their furnaces

we gave them
the fruits
of this land

they poisoned
the rivers
with mercury

yet we survived
the slaughter
of our days

and now
we face them
in this final battle

to save
our lives
the lives of all

desierto/desert
give us
your strength

viento/wind
blow into us
your courage

madre agua
guide us with
your tender ways

carnalitos
y carnalitas —
brothers
and sisters
don't be afraid

las flores
las plumas —
the flowers
the feathers
are on our side!

El amor no existe

el amor
no existe
me dices

mentira
que haya
amantes

es puro
invento
de tontos

me explicas
ocultando
tu sorpresa

al ver
en el cristal
del café

a nuestras
dos sombras
abrazándose

Love Doesn't Exist

love
doesn't exist
you tell me

it's a lie
that there are
lovers

the pure
invention
of fools

you explain
concealing
your surprise

as you notice
in the window
of the café

both of our
shadows
embracing

Mis manos	My Hands
yo no tengo	I have no
otros ojos	other eyes
que mis manos	than my hands
ni más boca	nor more of a mouth
corazón	a heart
que mis manos	than my hands
temblorosas	trembling
se acercan	they close in
hacia ti	on you
en lo oscuro de	in the dark of night
la noche te ven	they see you
te hablan	speak to you

Mi cama

es la balsa
en que navego
todas las noches
buscando salvar
los restos
de mi naufragio

es el muelle
de mi pobre
puerto
que con ansias
espera regresen
los marineros

es mi isla
perdida
mi alberca
mi cuadrilátero
lo que me queda
de árabe

es mi último
refugio
mi nido
mi tumba:
el único altar
de mi casa

My Bed

it is the raft
on which I sail
every night
looking to salvage
the remains
of my shipwreck

it is the dock
in my poor
harbor
longing
for the return
of sailors

it is my lost
island
my cistern
my wrestling ring
the trace of Arab
left in me

it is my last
refuge
my nest
my tomb —
the only altar
in my home

Orden en la casa

me reclamas
porque dejo
toallas húmedas
sobre la cama

todas las cosas
tienen su lugar
me aleccionas
recogiendo

los libros
amontonados
en la mesa
de la cocina

yo me apresuro
y cubro
con mi cuerpo
los calzones

que relucen
como sonrisa
sobre el sofá
rojo de la sala

Order in the Home

you complain
because I leave
damp towels
on the bed

all things
have their place
you lecture me
gathering

the pile
of books
off the kitchen
table

I hurry
and cover
with my body
the underwear

that gleams
like a smile
on the red
living-room sofa

Mi pelo	My Hair
cuando	when
me conociste	you met me
mi pelo era	my hair was
negro como	black like
el más negro	the blackest
lienzo	canvas
con tu pelo	with your hair
haré finos	I'll make the finest
pinceles	paintbrushes
me decías	you would tell me
mordiéndome	biting
las orejas	my ears
y yo corría	and I would run
con mi pelo	with my black
negro suelto	hair loose
como potro	like a colt
reluciendo	its black mane
su negra crin	shining
con tus canas	with your gray hair
ahora hice	I've made now
una larga soga	a long rope
me dices	you tell me
amarrándome	wrapping it
el cuello	around my neck

Mis muertos

un día lluvioso
me dieron lástima
y los deje entrar
desde entonces
mis muertos y yo
somos inseparables

me acompañan
adonde yo vaya —
unos son alegres
otros pensativos
todos me cuentan
historias increíbles

hay uno simpático
que al hablarme
me agarra las manos
el pobre insiste:
"mírame bien porque
éste que ves eres tú"

My Dead

one rainy day
I felt pity
and let them in
since then
me and my dead
are inseparable

they tag along
wherever I go —
some are cheerful
others pensive
all tell me
incredible stories

the good-natured one
when speaking to me
grabs hold of my hands
the poor guy insists —
"take a good long look
it's *you* you're looking at"

Carta a América

perdona
la tardanza
en escribirte

a nosotros
nos dejaron
pocas letras

en tu casa
nos tocó
ser tapetes

a veces
de pared
pero casi

siempre
estuvimos
en el piso

también
te servimos
de mesa

de lámpara
de espejo
de juguete

si algo
te causamos
fue risa

Letter to America

pardon
the lag
in writing you

we were left
with few
words

in your home
we were cast
as rugs

sometimes
on walls
though we

were almost
always
on the floor

we served
you as
a table

a lamp
a mirror
a toy

if anything
we made
you laugh

en tu cocina	in your kitchen
nos hiciste	we became
otro sartén	another pan
todavía	even now
como sombra	as a shadow
nos usas	you use us
nos temes	you fear us
nos gritas	you yell at us
nos odias	you hate us
nos tiras	you shoot us
nos lloras	you mourn us
nos niegas	you deny us
y a pesar	and despite
de todo	everything
nosotros	we
seguimos	continue
siendo	being
nosotros	us
América	America
entiende	understand
de una vez:	once and for all—
somos	we are
las entrañas	the insides
de tu cuerpo	of your body
en la cara	our faces
reflejamos	reflect
tu futuro	your future

Loma Prieta

Loma Prieta

¿quién
te mordió
las chiches
Madre?

Loma Prieta

who dared
to bite
your nipples
Mother?

Memorial

do towns
suffer
like people
heart attacks

do buildings
get scared
too and try
to run

do steel
frames
get twisted
out of pain

do windows
break
because
they can't cry

do walls let
themselves go
just
like that

and lie on
sidewalks
waiting
to be revived

is this how
old places
give birth
to new places?

Oportunidad	Chance
la ciudad	the city
no tiene	has no
electricidad	electricity
"¡qué	"what
pesadilla!"	a nightmare!"
digo yo	I say
"una oportunidad	"a chance
para contar	to count
estrellas"	stars"
dices tú	you say
apuntando	pointing
al cielo	to the sky

Gatherers

to Sue, Fredy, Little Marisela,
Chris, Cruz, Jaime, and Javier

in front of
our house
we formed
a circle of
chairs

we waited
for the night
listening
to news
on the radio

each
aftershock
brought us
closer
and closer

sometimes
we stared
at each other
sometimes
we laughed

in hours
we went
back maybe
a thousand
years

we were
now
a small band
of mystic
gatherers

Pobres poetas

a Miguel Ángel Flores

por las calles
rondan poetas
como pajaritos
caídos del nido

dan con los postes
del alumbrado
que de pronto
les salen al paso

ceremoniosos
les piden permiso
a las bancas vacías
de los parques

nadie sabe ni ellos
mismos por qué
en los hombros
les brotan alas

un día quizá usen
por fin esa llave
que desde siempre
traen en el bolsillo

Poor Poets

to Miguel Ángel Flores

poets go astray
on the streets
like chicks fallen
from their nest

they bump into
light posts that
without warning
cross their path

courteous as ever
they ask empty
park benches
for permission to sit

nobody knows
not even they
why wings sprout
on their shoulders

maybe one day
they'll finally use
that key they carry
forever in their pocket

Víctima del sismo

amor mío
que tus manos
me desentierren
que tus besos
me revivan

que me mojen
tus ojos
que me cubran
tus caricias
y tu vaho

que mi pecho
sienta
el latido de
tu corazón
y tu furia

que todavía
muerda
en la boca
tu flor
y tu esencia

que muerto
siga mirando
tu rostro
que tu cuerpo
sea mi tumba

que quede así
víctima del
terremoto
del amor
y la pasión

Lamentario	Lamentary
es triste	how sad
ser vaso	to be a glass
y nunca	that never
llenarse	gets filled
ser puerta	a door
y siempre	that stays
quedarse	forever
trancada	locked
ser cama	a bed that
sentirse	feels like
mortaja	a casket
no lecho	not a bedstead
es triste	how sad
ser uno	to be one
y nunca	and never
sumar dos	add to two
ser ave	a bird
sin nido	without a nest
ser santo	a saint with
sin vela	no candlelight
ser solo	to be alone
y vivir	and live on
soñando	dreaming up
abrazos	embraces

Blessed the Big One

wouldn't it be better
to never get
power back

to have idle
fridges TV sets
microwave ovens

to never again
run rivers
inside plumbing

wouldn't it make
a difference
to let cars rust

to walk around
to ride bikes
instead of freeways

wouldn't it give us
at least a chance
to find a way

to heal ourselves
to let Earth
breathe a little

how many trees
how many animals
how many of us

wouldn't give thanks
for being saved
by the Big One

Tambores

to Javier Muñiz, Raúl Rivera, José Luis Pérez,
y toda la palomilla drumming at Fort Mason,
San Francisco, December 15, 1989

bring us
our ancient
roots

the language
of lakes
and birds

our first
breath
of fire

teach us
the song
of the sea

let us
see with
our hands

touch again
el ombligo
de la tierra

First-Person Eulogy

I lost my home
my china my store
I broke my arm
the back of my neck

I didn't know
what to do
I ran I froze
I cried I laughed

I thought about
the children
I panicked I prayed
I was helpless

I saw the eyes
of the woman
buried at Ford's
I saw myself dying

I was so worried
I felt guilty
I didn't sleep
I snored

I waited and waited
and he never came
I ate all the cookies
I lost my appetite

I read all the papers
I was bored I missed

school I didn't give a damn
about the World Series

I volunteered myself
I overcharged for water
and ice — what the hell
I was rude I was generous

I wrote lots of letters
I finished my projects
I was glued to the TV
I got drunk I got high

I cleaned my room
I was hungry I was cold
I was sad I was angry
I ached all over

I was the looter
and the fireman
I was the preacher
and the hooker

the politician
the grabber of
headlines and
just another loner

I was the dreamer
the listener
the heartbroken
the mouthpiece

strangers became
familiar — this pronoun
I for once included
each and every one

Vision

to Christopher Funkhouser

there were
no houses
no streets
no fences

only pines
and meadows
tall grasses
and seagulls

on the same
spot where
my bed
once stood

there was
a sea lion
winking
at me

Snake Poems
An Aztec Invocation

Lo cierto es que las más o casi todas las adoraciones actuales o
acciones idolátricas, que ahora hallamos, y a lo que podemos
juzgar, son las mismas que acostumbraban sus antepasados,
tienen su raíz y fundamento formal en tener ellos fe que las
nubes son ángeles y dioses, capaces de adoración, y lo mismo
juzgan a los vientos, por lo cual creen que en todas partes de la
tierra habitan, como en las lomas, valles y quebradas. Lo mismo
creen de los ríos, lagunas y manantiales, pues a todo lo dicho
ofrecen cera e incienso.

—Hernando Ruiz de Alarcón,
*Tratado de las supersticiones y costumbres gentílicas que hoy
viven entre los indios naturales desta Nueva España* (1629)

What is certain is that most or almost all present-day forms of
worship or idolatrous actions, which we now come across (and,
from what we can judge, they are the same ones their ancestors
customarily used), have their roots and formal basis in their
belief that the clouds are angels and gods worthy of worship.
They think the same of the winds because they believe these
forces live everywhere, in the hills, mountains, valleys, and
ravines. They believe the same of the rivers, lakes, and springs
because they offer wax and incense to all the above.

—Hernando Ruiz de Alarcón,
*Treatise on the Superstitions and Heathen Customs That Today
Live among the Indians Native to This New Spain* (1629)

Los flecheros llaman cuatro veces a
los venados, repitiendo cuatro veces
esta palabra *tahui,* que hoy no hay
quien la entienda, y luego gritan
cuatro veces a semejanza del león.

The archers call four times to the deer,
repeating four times this word *tahui,*
which nobody understands today,
and then they cry out four times
like a puma.

—Ruiz de Alarcón (1:2)

Four Directions

WEST

we are
salmons
looking for
our womb

NORTH

eagles
flying
the Sun
in our beak

EAST

coyotes
calling
each other
in the Moon

SOUTH

we turn
into snakes
by eating
chile

Hernando Ruiz
de Alarcón
(1587–1646)

eras tú
al que buscabas
Hernando

hurgando
en los rincones
de las casas

semillas
empolvadas
de *ololiuhqui*

eras tú
al que engañabas
y aprehendías

eras tú
el que preguntaba
y respondía

dondequiera
mirabas moros
con trinchete

y ante
tanto dolor
tanta muerte

Hernando Ruiz
de Alarcón
(1587–1646)

it was you
you were looking for
Hernando

searching
every house
corner

for some
dusty seeds
of *ololiuhqui*

it was you
whom you tricked
and apprehended

it was you
who both questioned
and responded

everywhere
you saw Moors
with long knives

and in front of
so much sorrow
so much death

un conquistador
conquistado
fuiste

sacerdote
soñador
cruz parlante

condenando
te salvaste
al transcribir

acaso
sin saber
el cielo

soy yo
el de tu cepa
el de tu sueño

este *cenzontle*
del monte:
tu mañana

you became
a conquered
conqueror

priest
dreamer
speaking cross

condemning
you saved yourself
by transcribing

maybe
without knowing
the heavens

I am
from your tree
from your dream

this *cenzontle* bird
in the wilderness—
your tomorrow

In the Middle of the Night

sobs
woke me

I got up
and saw

myself
in a corner

crying

Shame

I washed
my arms
scrubbed
my face

powder
soap
fell from
my hands

but
my skin
only got
redder

I was
just
another
itching

brown
boy
getting
ready

for school

Mestizo

my name
is not
Francisco

there is
an Arab
within me

who prays
five times
each day

behind
my Roman
nose

there is
a Phoenician
smiling

my eyes
still see
Sevilla

but
my mouth
is Olmec

my dark
hands are
Toltec

my cheekbones
fierce
Chichimec

my feet
recognize
no border

no rule
no code
no lord

for this
wanderer's
heart

Matriarch

my dark
grandmother

would brush
her long hair

seated out
on her patio

even ferns
would bow

to her splendor
and her power

Tonalamatl / Spirit Book

pages
whisper
sigh
sing

glyphs
dance
left
to right

I follow
the drums
the scent
the stairs

mountain
mist
sprays
my hair

I learn
to undo
what is
done

an ancient
jaguar
roars
at my face

I start
singing
all kinds
of flowers

Songs

xochitl
flower
flor

To Those Who Have Lost Everything

crossed
in despair
many deserts
full of hope

carrying
their empty
fists of sorrow
everywhere

mouthing
a bitter night
of shovels
and nails

"you're nothing
you're shit
your home's
nowhere" —

mountains
will speak
for you

rain
will flesh
your bones

green again
among ashes
after a long fire

started in
a fantasy island
some time ago

turning
Natives
into aliens

Never Alone

always
this caressing
Wind

this Earth
whispering
to our feet

this boundless
desire
of being

grass
tree
corazón

Nomatca Nehuatl

I myself:
the mountain
the ocean
the breeze
the flame

the thorn
the serpent
the feather
the Moon
the Sun

the sister
the brother
the mother
the father
the other

the ground
the seed
the chant
the cloud
the flower

the deer
the hunter
the arrow
the neck
the blood

the dead
the dancing
the house
the quake
the lizard

the island
the shell
the collar
the star
the lover

the search
the face
the dream
the heart
the voice:

nomatca nehuatl!

Journey

Ruiz de Alarcón (I:4)

In each village, there was a large, well-kept courtyard, something
like a church, from where the *tlamacazqui,* the old priest, would
send the *tlamaceuhque,* the penitent, on his rite of passage. Each
individual began his pilgrimage by bringing green firewood to
this courtyard for the elders, who were distinguished by a long
lock of hair. This lock of hair was also a sign among Indians of
great captains and warriors called *tlacauhque.*

During the night, the elder, squatting on a low stone seat and
holding in his hands a large *tecomate,* a gourd vessel, full of
tenexiete, tobacco with lime, would then address *tlamaceuhque,*
ordering him to go to the forest, home of Tlaticpaque, Lord of
the Wilderness. The words the elder spoke were:

xoniciuhtiuh	hurry off
nocomichic	bottom of my vessel
noxocoyo	my youngest child
noceuhteuh	my only one
mazan cana	beware of delaying
timaahuiltitiuh	somewhere —
nimitzchixtiyez	I'll be watching you
nican niyetlacuitica	here smoking my tobacco pipe
nitlacuepalotica	keeping up the fire
nitlachixtica	I'm watching you
izca	behold! —
nimitzcualtia	I give you
tichuicaz …	food to carry …

91

nican nitlachixtica	here I'm watching you—
nOxomoco	I, *Oxomoco*
niHuehueh	I, the Ancient One
niCipactonal	I, *Cipactonal*

Traveler's Prayer

Ruiz de Alarcón (II:1)

nomatca nehuatl	I myself
niQuetzalcoatl	I, Quetzalcoatl
niMatl	I, the Hand
ca nehuatl niYaotl	indeed I, the Warrior
niMoquequeloatzin	I, the Mocker
atle ipan nitlamati ...	I respect nothing ...
tla xihualhuian	come forth
tlamacazque	spirits
tonatiuh iquizayan	from the sunset
tonatiuh icalaquiyan	from the sunrise
in ixquichca nemi	anywhere you dwell
in yolli	as animals
in patlantinemi	as birds
in ic nauhcan	from the four directions
niquintzatzilia	I call you
ic axcan yez ...	to my grip ...
tla xihuallauh	come forth
Ce-Tecpatl	knife
tezzohuaz	to be stained
titlapallohuaz	with blood
tla xihuallauh	come forth
Tlaltecuin	cross my path

Midnight Water Song

the eagle's
wing is
my fan

my people's
past is
my staff

my pounding
heart
the only drum

this nightfall
this sagebrush
this cedar smoke

tumbleweeds
rattle
as I sing

of peyote's
flowering rain
in the desert

Ololiuhqui

to Bárbara García

seeds
of wisdom
divine eyes
of serpents

teach us
to read
again
the sky

buttons of
the infinite
skirt
of stars

turn us
into
hummingbirds
kissing flowers

lead us
back
to the lap
of our Mother

Morning Ritual

I fold
kiss
carry

my life
inside
my pocket

Chicome-Xochitl / Seven Flower

deer
father

all
stems

pointing
stars

For Planting Corn

Ruiz de Alarcón (III:4)

nomatca nehuatl	I myself
nitlamacazqui	Spirit in Flesh:
tla xihualhuian	hear me, *Tonacacihuatl*
nohueltiuh	elder sister
Tonacacihuatl	Lady of Our Flesh
tla xihualhuian	hear me, *Tlalteuctli*
Tlalteuctli	Mother Earth
ye momacpalco	on your open hand
nocontlalia	I am setting down
nohueltiuh	my elder sister
Tonacacihuatl	*Tonacacihuatl*
ahmo timopinauhtiz	don't shame yourself
ahmo tihuexcapehuaz	don't grumble
ahmo tihuexcatlatlacoz	don't laugh at us
cuix quin moztla	tomorrow
cuix quin huiptla	or the day after
in ixco icpac nitlachiaz	I want to see again
in nohueltiuh	the face of my elder sister
Tonacacihuatl	*Tonacacihuatl*
niman iciuhca	let her stand
in tlalticpac hualquizaz	on the ground

in nicmahuizoz	I shall greet
in nictlapaloz	I shall honor
in nohueltiuh	my elder sister
Tonacacihuatl	*Tonacacihuatl*

Rueda víbora

habrá soy eres somos este futuro vuelto pasado todo lo que hubo lo que hubo hay

Snake Wheel

was is will be I you we are this future turned past all that once

Ode to Tomatoes

they make
friends
anywhere

red
smiles
in salads

tender
young
generous

hot
salsa
dancers

round
cardinals
of the kitchen

hard
to imagine
cooking

without
first asking
their blessings!

Potent Seeds

few corn
kernels
enough

to turn
anger
around

Una de las cosas de que usan por medicina a que atribuyen parte del efecto, son unos granos de maíz que tienen su asiento en principio y nacimiento de la espiga o mazorca, y tales granos tienen las puntillas contrarias al nacimiento, al revés y a la parte contraria que las demás de la dicha mazorca, y a esta contrariedad atribuyen el efecto contrario en la inclinación y voluntad en cuanto a la afición y odio. A estos granos de maíz aplican la segunda parte de este medio, que son las palabras con que a su juicio conjurando los maíces, les dan nueva fuerza y virtud para conseguir el efecto del trueque que pretenden.... Hecho este conjuro para aplicar la medicina, moliendo el maíz conjurado, hacen de él alguna bebida al uso de esta tierra, como es atole y cacao, y dánselo a beber al que pretenden trueque la voluntad o afecto.

Among the things they use for medicine against anger are the corn kernels that are located at the beginning and root of the spike or ear. These kernels have their points contrary to their root—backward and in the opposite direction to the rest on that particular ear. It is to this inverted position that the Indians attribute the contrary effect that the incantation and spell have on affection and hatred. To the corn kernels they apply these words, which they believe give the kernels added strength and power and allow them to effect the change they seek.... After the conjured corn has been ground, it is administered orally as either atole or chocolate to the person whose will or affection they want to change.

—Hernando Ruiz de Alarcón (IV:1)

Against Anger

Ruiz de Alarcón (IV:1)

tla xihualhuian	come forth
Tlazopilli	*Tlazopilli*
Centeotl	*Centeotl*
ticcehuiz	you will calm down
cozauhqui yollotli	the yellow heart
quizaz	the green anger
xoxouhqui tlahuelli	the yellow anger
cozauhqui tlahuelli	will come out
nicquixtiz	I shall make it leave
nictotocaz	I shall chase it away —
nitlamacazqui	I, Spirit in Flesh
ninahualteuctli	I, the Enchanter
niquitiz tlamazcazqui	through this drink
Pahtecatl	Medicine Spirit
Yollohcuepcatzin	will change this heart

In Ixtli In Yollotl / Face and Heart

to Juan Pablo Gutiérrez

may our ears
hear
what nobody
wants to hear

may our eyes
see
what everyone
wants to hide

may our mouths
speak
our true faces
and hearts

may our arms
be branches
that give shade
and joy

let us be a drizzle
a sudden storm
let us get wet
in the rain

let us be the key
the hand the door
the kick the ball
the road

let us arrive
as children
to this huge
playground—

the universe

For Finding Affection

Ruiz de Alarcón (IV:2)

Tezcatepeyec	on Mirror Mountain
nenamicoyan	the place of encounters
nicihuanotzca	I call for a woman
nicihuacuica	I sing out for her
nonnentlamati	crying up
nihualnentlamati	crying down
ye noconhuica	already at my side
in nohueltiuth	my elder sister
in Xochiquetzal	*Xochiquetzal*
Ce-Coatl ica	with One Serpent
apantiuitz	as her mantle
Ce-Coatl	with One Serpent
cuitlalpitihuitz	as her belt
tzonilpitihuitz	as ribbon in her hair
ye yalhua	since yesterday
ye huiptla	the day before
ica nichoca	I wept
ica ninentlamati	I cried
ca mach nelli teotl	she is a true goddess
ca mach nelli mahuiztic	she is a true power
cuix quin moztla	tomorrow?
cuix quin huiptla	the day after?
niman aman	right now!

nomatca nehuatl	I myself
niTelpochtli	I, the Youth
niYaotl	I, the Warrior —
no nitonac	I sunshine
no nitlathuic	I dawn
cuix zan cana onihualla	risen from nowhere?
cuix zan cana onihualquiz	born from nowhere?
ompa onihualla	I have risen, I was born
ompa onihualquiz ...	of a woman's flower ...

The words that belong here, even though somewhat disguised,
are omitted out of concern for modest and chaste ears. (Ruiz de
Alarcón's note)

ca mach nelli teotl	she is a true goddess
ca mach nelli mahuiztic	she is a true power
cuix quin moztla	will I find her
cuix quin huiptla	tomorrow?
niquittaz	the day after?
niman aman	right now!
nomatca nehuatl	I myself
niTelpochtli	I, the Youth
niYaotl	I, the Warrior
cuix nelli niYaotl	am I truly warlike?
ahmo nelli niYaotl	I am not truly at war —
zan niCihuayotl	I'm of a woman's womb

For Love

enchanted
words
at dawn

a handful
of flowers
and stars

Tonantzin

Madre
¿aquí estás
con nosotros?

enjuáganos
el sudor
las lágrimas

Coatlicue
tú que reinas
sobre las serpientes

Chalchiuhcueye
haznos
el favor

Citlalcueye
que nos guíen
tus estrellas

Guadalupe
sé nuestra aurora
nuestra esperanza

¡bandera
y fuego de
nuestra rebelión!

Tonantzin

Mother
are you here
with us?

wipe up
our sweat
our tears

Coatlicue
you who rule
over snakes

Chalchiuhcueye
grant us
our request

Citlalcueye
let your stars
guide us

Guadalupe
be our dawn
our hope

the flag
and fire of
our rebellion!

Cihuacoatl

in the barrios
La Llorona
has run out
of tears

Working Hands

we clean
your room

we do
your dishes

a footnote
for you

but hands
like these

one day
will write

the main text
of this land

In Xochitl In Cuicatl

In Xochitl In Cuicatl

cada árbol	every tree
un hermano	a brother
cada monte	every hill
una pirámide	a pyramid
un oratorio	a holy spot
cada valle	every valley
un poema	a poem
in xochitl	*in xochitl*
in cuicatl	*in cuicatl*
flor y canto	flower and song
cada nube	every cloud
una plegaria	a prayer
cada gota	every drop
de lluvia	of rain
un milagro	a miracle
cada cuerpo	every body
una orilla	a seashore
al mar	a memory
un olvido	at once lost
encontrado	and found
todos juntos:	we all together —
luciérnagas	fireflies
de la noche	in the night
soñando	dreaming up
el cosmos	the cosmos

No Golden Gate for Us

Silence

I smell
silence
everywhere

clean
nice homes
smell

banks
smell
so do malls

no deodorant
odorizer
or perfume

can put way
this stink
of silence

The X in My Name

the poor
signature of
my illiterate
and peasant self

giving away
all rights
in a deceptive
contract for life

Callejeros	Streetwise
sólo	only
estos perros	these dogs
saben	know about
del dolor	the grief
de las calles	of streets
a oscuras	after dark
mientras	while beds
en las casas	squeak
crujen camas	inside homes
ellos afuera	they trace
rastrean	oblivion
el olvido	outside
los rebeldes	forever
de siempre	rebellious
los desolados	desperados
no ladran	they don't bark
ni gruñen	or growl
a los ladrones	at thieves
lo contrario—	*au contraire*—
chisguetean	they spray
los muros	the walls
de los bares	of bars
los bancos	banks
las iglesias	churches

Californian Missions

I visit
old missions
on the Day
of the Dead

San Diego
San Gabriel
San Juan Bautista
San Rafael

Santa Clara
Santa Barbara
Santa Inés
Santa Cruz

it almost always
rains tears
white walls
begin to sweat

I keep
lighting candles
hoping for a
big Indian fire

L.A. Prayer

April 1992

something
was wrong
when buses
didn't come

streets
were
no longer
streets

how easy
hands
became
weapons

blows
gunfire
rupturing
the night

the more
we run
the more
we burn

o god
show us
the way
lead us

spare us
from ever
turning into
walking

matches
amidst
so much
gasoline

Soother

I bite
tongue
your erect
dark nipples

so
your heart
won't become
another fist

Amor zurdo

pueden
mandarme
a la cárcel

señalarme
reírse
en mi cara

correrme
de por
aquí

apedrearme
hasta
morir

borrar
todo rastro
mío

pero no
pueden hacer
que deje de

tocar
acariciar
quererte

Amor zurdo

they can
throw me
in jail

point
laugh
in my face

run me
out
of town

stone me
to
death

write me
off
any record

but can't
keep me
from

touching
caressing
loving you

Seer

I sweep
and clean
my house

I burn
the trash
get rid
of obstacles

my house
now has
no walls
no anger
or sorrow

I am resting—
my *hamaca*
is a canoe
crossing
the Milky Way

"Mexican" Is Not a Noun

to forty-six UC Santa Cruz students and
seven faculty arrested in Watsonville for
showing solidarity with two thousand
striking cannery workers who were mostly
Mexican women, October 27, 1985

"Mexican"
is not
a noun
or an
adjective

"Mexican"
is a life
long
low-paying
job

a check
mark on
a welfare
police
form

more than
a word
a nail in
the soul
but

it hurts
it points
it dreams
it offends
it cries

it moves
it strikes
it burns
just like
a verb

Continental	Continental
San Francisco, Califas	*San Francisco, Califas*
las calles	the streets
de mi barrio	of my barrio
La Misión	La Misión
dan a	lead to
Tegucigalpa	Tegucigalpa
Guatemala	Guatemala
Managua	Managua
San Salvador	San Salvador
el mismo	the same
olor a pobre	air of poverty
el mismo pan	the same daily
de cada día	bread
la misma	the same
música	music
cosquilleando	tickling us
las entrañas	inside
y la vida	and life
colgada	hanging
como piñata	like a piñata
de un hilo	by a thread
y palos	and blows
muchos palos	many blows
dondequiera	everywhere
muchos muertos	lots of dead

por eso aquí
el café deja
anillos de luto
en las tazas

por eso mismo
las banderas
aquí se usan
de mantel —

por las calles
de mi barrio
anda suelto todo
un continente

that's why
coffee leaves
mourning rings
in cups

and for this
reason flags
up here are used
as tablecloths —

through the streets
of my barrio
roams a whole
continent

Casa materna	Maternal Home
toqué	I knocked
a la puerta	at the door
de mi casa	of my home
de negro	a lady
una señora	in black
salió	answered
una sombra	a shadow
empuñando	clenching
una escoba	a broom
sin palabras	speechless
me quedé	I did nothing
mirando	but stare
donde	where
se canceló	my childhood
mi infancia	was canceled
después	after
del portazo	the door slam
seguí ahí	I just stood
parado	there
llorando	weeping
por dentro	inside

Isla Mujeres

por qué
no entrar
a cualquier
casa de
pescador
y decir:
"ya llegué"

y una vez
sentados
a nuestras
anchas
suspirar:
"es una larga
historia …"

Isla Mujeres

why not
just go
into any
fisherman's
house
and say:
"I'm home"

and once
seated
at our
ease
sigh:
"it's a long
story …"

De amor oscuro / Of Dark Love

English translations by Francisco Aragón

¡ay voz secreta del amor oscuro!
¡ay balido sin lanas! ¡ay herida!
¡ay aguja sin hiel, camelia hundida!
¡ay corriente sin mar, ciudad sin muro!...

—Federico García Lorca, *Sonetos del amor oscuro (1935)*

I

para este amor nunca ha habido sol,
como loca flor, en lo oscuro brota,
es, a la vez, corona de espinas y
guirnalda de primavera en la sien

fuego, herida y amarguísimo fruto,
pero también brisa y manantial,
una mordida al alma: tu aliento,
un tronco en la corriente: tu pecho

hazme caminar sobre el agua turbia,
sé el hacha que rompa este candado,
el rocío que haga llorar los árboles

si mudo quedo al besar tus muslos
es que mi corazón con afán busca
entre tu carne un nuevo amanecer

I

there has never been sunlight for this love,
like a crazed flower it buds in the dark,
is at once a crown of thorns and
a spring garland around the temples

a fire, a wound, the bitterest fruit,
but a breeze as well, a source of water,
your breath—a bite to the soul,
your chest—a tree trunk in the current

make me walk on the turbid waters,
be the ax that breaks this lock,
the dew that weeps from trees

if I become mute kissing your thighs,
it's that my heart eagerly
searches your flesh for a new dawn

IV

tus manos son dos martillos que clavan
y desclavan alegres la mañana,
tiernos puños desdoblados de tierra,
dulces pencas de plátanos pequeños

tus manos huelen a las zarzamoras
que cosechas en los campos que roban
tu sudor a dos dólares el bote,
son duras, tibias, jóvenes y sabias

azadones que traen pan a las mesas,
oscuras piedras que al chocar dan luz,
gozo, sostén y ancla del mundo entero

yo las venero como relicarios
porque como gaviotas anidadas
me consuelan, me alegran, me defienden

IV

your hands are two hammers that joyfully
nail down and pry up the morning,
tender fists that unfold from earth,
sweet bunches of small bananas

your hands smell of the blackberries
you harvest in the fields that steal
your sweat at two dollars a bucket,
they are hard, warm, young, and wise

hoes that bring bread to the tables,
dark stones that give light when struck,
pleasure, support, anchor of the world

I worship them as reliquaries
because like nesting seagulls
they console, delight, defend me

VI

al dormir te vuelves un continente,
largo, misterioso, sin descubrir,
tus piernas: cordilleras apartadas,
van circundando valles y cañadas

la noche se resbala por tus párpados,
tu respirar: vaivén de olas de mar,
en la cama te extiendes mansamente
como un delfín alojado en la playa

tu boca: boca de volcán saciado,
leño perfumado, ¿en qué fuego ardes?
estás tan cerca y a la vez, tan lejos

mientras duermes como lirio a mi lado,
yo me deshago, invoco a la luna:
ahora soy el perro guardián de tu sueño

VI

asleep you become a continent—
long, mysterious, undiscovered,
the mountain ranges of your legs
encircle valleys and ravines

night slips past your eyelids,
your breath—the swaying of the sea,
you lie peacefully on the bed
like a beached dolphin

your mouth—the mouth of a sated volcano,
o fragrant timber, what fire burns you?
you are so near, and yet so far

as you doze like a lily at my side,
I undo myself and invoke the moon—
now I am this dog guarding your sleep

VII

me gusta caminar junto a tu lado,
ir pisando en el malecón tu sombra,
dejar que tus pasos marquen mis pasos,
seguirte como barco remolcado

ajustando mis pies en las huellas
que como puma dejas en la playa,
quiero ser la toalla con que te secas,
donde te extiendes a tomar el sol

qué suerte la del cinturón que abraza
tu cintura, la del cristo que cuelga
de una cadena entre tus pectorales

qué alegría llegar como peine diario
a oler la manaña en tus cabellos
y en vez de peinarte, despeinarte

VII

I like to walk beside you, treading
your shadow along the way,
letting your steps mark my steps,
follow you like a boat being towed—

fitting my feet in the footprints
you leave like a puma on the sand,
I want to be the towel that dries you,
the one you spread to sunbathe

how lucky! the belt that gets to hug
your waist, the crucifix that hangs
from a chain on your chest!

what joy! to arrive every day as a comb
and smell the morning in your hair
but rather than comb, uncomb you

X

"dos caminos hay en el mundo: el verse
un día en un espejo o el nunca llegar
a verse de veras, verse es vivir,
no verse, estar muerto," me aleccionas

"mírame, yo soy más que mi mirada,
más que una sonrisa en plena calle,
más que todos los horizontes juntos:
el que te mira es más que ése que miras"

"al verme en ti, descubro lo que soy,
así quiero que tú te veas en mí:
que al mírarme te mires mirándote"

"mírame que me estoy mirando en ti,
mírame que tú eres espejo mío,
mírame que yo quiero ser el tuyo"

X

"there are two ways in the world: to see
yourself one day in the mirror, or never see
your true self-image, to see yourself is to live,
not seeing yourself is death," you tell me

"look at me, I am more than my look,
more than a passing smile on a street,
more than piled horizons, the one who looks
at you is more than the one you look at"

"seeing myself in you, I discover who I am,
I want you to see yourself likewise in me:
looking at me, see yourself looking at you"

"look at me, for I see myself in you,
look at me, for you are my mirror,
look at me, I want to be yours"

XII

por tu ventana me asomo otra vez
al mundo que algo tiene diferente,
quizás hayan florecido los campos,
o tal vez hayan nacido más estrellas

las olas me acarician, delirantes,
los pies, algo nuevo, desconocido,
me susurran también los crepúsculos,
en todo hallo tu aroma, tu figura

tú estás entre los pinos milenarios,
tras la neblina en las peñas marinas,
en medio de la tarde más sombría

imposible borrar tu regocijo
de mis ojos, de mi triste boca,
así eres: el universo hecho carne

XII

once again I look out your window
and the world looks oddly different,
maybe the fields have blossomed,
or perhaps more stars have been born

delirious waves caress my feet,
something new, unknown,
sunsets whisper in my ear as well,
everywhere I find your odor, your shape

you are among old-growth pines,
in the fog along the coastal rocks,
around the most somber of afternoons

impossible to wipe away your joy
from my eyes, from my sad mouth —
you are the universe made flesh

XIV

¿cómo consolar al hombre más solo
de la tierra? ¿cómo aliviar su pena?
¿cómo llamar a su puerta atrancada
y decirle al oído embocado de alma:

"hermano, la guerra ya ha terminado:
todos, por fin, salimos vencedores,
sal, goza los campos liberados,
la explotación es cosa del pasado"?

¿qué hacer cuando regrese malherido
con alambre de púas entre las piernas?
¿cómo encarar sus ojos que denuncian:

"hermano, el mundo sigue igual:
los pobres todavía somos presa fácil:
el amor, si no es de todos, no basta"?

XIV

how to console the loneliest man
on earth? how to relieve his pain?
how to call through his bolted door
and have one's soul speak to his ear:

"brother, the war is now over —
all of us in the end emerged victors,
go forth and enjoy the liberated fields,
exploitation is a thing of the past"?

what to do when he returns, wounded
with barbed wire between his legs?
how to face his eyes accusing:

"brother, it's business as usual —
we the poor are still likely prey — love,
if not for everyone, isn't enough"?

Sonnets to Madness and Other Misfortunes

Sonetos a la locura y otras penas

English Translations by Francisco Aragón

Nuevo día

amanécete mundo
entre mis brazos
que el peso de
tu ternura me despierte

New Day

wake in my arms
beloved world—
may your soft stir
awaken me

II

abrazarte quisiera, viento mío,
tu cuello de verano acariciar,
y besar y besar tu tersa frente
hasta evaporar todas las distancias

las colinas, los viñedos, el mar,
ligero los cargas sobre tu espalda
como joven amanecer de gozo,
capaz de convertir la noche en día

viento, ambiciono tu libertad,
la altura de montaña de tus ojos
esa lumbre que atiza calles, lechos

viento, ¿no ves mis manos llamaradas?
¿no sientes el calor de mis entrañas?
yo también, en las venas, llevo fuego

II

I want to embrace you, dear wind,
stroke your summer neck,
and kiss and kiss your smooth face
till all distances disappear

the hills, vineyards, the sea
are borne lightly on your shoulders,
like dawn's youthful pleasure
you can turn night into day

wind, I aspire to your freedom,
to see mountaintops with your eyes,
that blaze that rouses streets and beds

wind, don't you see my shimmering hands?
don't you feel the heat inside me?
I too, within my veins, carry fire

III

tus ojos me enseñan de nuevo a ver
como espejos de agua todo lo entienden,
no hay enigma que no puedan descifrar
pues le basta y sobra una mirada

tus ojos ven, escuchan, tocan, hablan,
son faros de luz que en el horizonte
alumbran la realidad de la vida
que queda más allá de las palabras

ahora me pongo a recorrer tu cuerpo,
le doy lectura a cada lunar tuyo
como signo de pausa y puntuación

cómo me gusta escribir en tu pecho,
tener por renglones a tus dorsales:
tú y yo somos tan pluma como página

III

your eyes show me how to see again
like mirrors of water, understanding all,
there's no mystery they can't solve —
a single glance is more than enough

your eyes see, listen, touch, speak,
are beacons on the horizon
shedding light on shades of life
beyond the reach of words

so I start to read your body,
pausing at every mole, as if
they were commas or periods

how I love to scribble on your chest,
use the muscles on your back as lines —
you and I are both page and pen

V

entonces las horas eran tan largas
que las mañanas duraban un día,
el sol del cielo era el único reloj
y el viento se sentaba a platicar

mientras la tierra así, recién llovida,
hacía cosquillas a los pies descalzos
y entre los árboles y las colinas,
las nubes jugaban a las escondidas

y las miradas como mariposas
volaban hacia sueños que un abrir
y cerrar de ojos ponía a flor de mano

entonces reír era lo más sensato,
gusto daba hasta llorar y la amistad
como la ternura se regalaba

V

back then hours were so long
mornings lasted entire days,
the sun in the sky our only clock,
and the wind sat down to chat

while the earth, damp with rain,
tickled the soles of bare feet,
and among the trees and hills,
clouds played hide and seek

and glances like butterflies
flitted toward dreams — in a
blink they'd alight in our hands

back then to laugh was common sense,
even to weep a pleasure, and friendship,
like tenderness, was a daily gift

VIII

escúchame como aquel eco perdido
y hallado en tu mañana de montaña,
mis palabras quieren ser para ti
alas blancas de gaviota en vuelo

moja tus pies en mi ojo de agua
que mi voz, feliz sale a borbotones,
recoge las azucenas que planté
en mi orilla verde para tu regazo

ven, abre la puerta de mi granero,
goza los arrozales cosechados
en la más remota de tus laderas

descansa bajo la sombra que dan
las ramas llenas de hojas de mis brazos,
soy la semilla que tu amor hizo árbol

VIII

listen to me like that echo lost
and found in your mountain dawn,
for you my words want to be
the white wings of a gliding gull

splash your feet in my spring,
for my voice bubbles with joy,
pick for your lap the lilies
planted along my green shore

come, open my barn doors,
relish the rice gathered in the most
hidden corners of your slopes

rest in the shade of the leafy branches
that are my arms—I am
the seed your love has made a tree

IX

y dije adiós como quien muerde el aire
mis palabras como platos frágiles
en el piso familiar se estrellaron,
verdes me despidieron las macetas

los retratos de la sala me dieron
su bendición y la puerta a la calle
me abrazó tan fuerte como mi madre:
"te vas, ya te fuiste, adónde irás"

y salí para un día llegar por fin
al mismo lugar donde había salido
pero todo estaba irreconocible

ya era otro, ahora daba yo más sombra,
más pena, entonces supe por qué
mi padre lloraba cuando llovía

IX

and I said good-bye as if biting the air,
my words, like fragile plates,
lay shattered on that floor,
potted plants waved *so long*

living-room portraits gave
their blessing as the front door
hugged me as tightly as my mother—
"you're going, you're gone, where will you go"

and out I went to one day arrive
to the place of my departure,
though everything had changed

as I had, my shadow longer, my pain
deeper, it was then I knew why
my father wept in the rain

XV

las palabras son llaves enmohecidas
que ya no abren puertas ni corazones,
son cuchillos sin filo que nos causan
una muerte pausada y dolorosa

son territorios recién conquistados
para vanagloria de reyes tontos,
son barcos encallados, oraciones
sin oír de multitudes naufragadas

llevan las camisas ensangrentadas,
el amargo sabor de violaciones,
enterrada en los ojos, la locura

son pan duro, remanso envenenado,
redes rotas, rejas de un pueblo entero,
tornillos que a un imperio lo desarman

XV

words are rusted keys
that open no doors or hearts,
unsharpened knives that bring us
a long and painful end

they're lands newly conquered
for the glory of foolish kings,
boats run aground, the unanswered
prayers of shipwrecked throngs

they wear bloodied shirts,
the bitter taste of violation —
madness deep in their eyes

they're stale bread, poisoned water,
torn nets, jails of an entire nation —
screws that can undo an empire

XVI

tras este lenguaje hay otro más antiguo,
ágil, huidizo como gato de barrio,
hogareño como el té de limón
de mi abuela en una tarde de lluvia

libre como sonrisa de autobús,
lo susurran sin palabras los amantes,
los niños se lo enseñan a sus perros
y lo vuelven a hablar los moribundos

lengua que no se da, sino se saca
a manazos, como el primer llorido
a un recién nacido en el hospital

aire resucitado en los pulmones,
canto y llanto, mueca y signo,
como cuña, abriéndonos la boca

XVI

beneath this language, there's another,
more ancient, agile, elusive
as an alley cat, cozy as lemon tea
my grandma made on rainy days

free as a big smile on a bus,
lovers, speechless, whisper it,
children teach it to their dogs,
the dead come back to utter it

language that isn't given
but slapped out, like
a newborn's first cry

air that is revived in the lungs,
song and sob, grimace and sign,
a wedge prying open our mouths

From the Other Side of Night
Del otro lado de la noche

Para nosotros

no hay
palabras

por eso
al encontrarnos

a veces
se nos hace

nudo
la garganta

For Us

there are
no words

that's why
sometimes

when we meet
a knot

ties up
our throats

Encuentro	Encounter
sin decir	saying
nada	nothing
nos decimos	we say
tanto	so much
los golpes	the bruises
por dentro	no one sees
las noches	the endless
sin fin	nights
con sólo	gazing
vernos	from a distance
ya estamos	already we're
abrazados	embracing
somos	we are
espejo	mirror
memoria	memory
umbral	threshold
extraños	strangers
que	who know
lo saben	all about
todo	each other

Del otro lado de la noche

From the Other Side of Night

qué decir
ante
el silencio

what to say
about
silence

las páginas
que se quedan
sin escribir

the pages
left
unwritten

los libros
en donde
todavía

the books
in which
we are yet

ni somos
ni estamos
ni existimos

to be
appear
exist

esta vida
condenada
al olvido

this life
condemned
to oblivion

aquí
nadie sabe
ni sabrá

here
nobody knows
nor will know

del mar
que llevamos
adentro

of the sea
we carry
within us

173

del fuego	of the fire
que encendemos	we ignite
con el cuerpo	with our bodies
del	from
otro lado	the other side
de la noche	of night

Afuera	Out
afuera	we're
estamos	out
aun	even
adentro	inside

Plegaria de amor	Love Plea
acógeme	love —
en tus brazos	take me
amor mío	into your arms
que soy	I am
el duelo	the mourning
de tu mediodía	of your noon
este río	this river
sin lecho	with no course
sin dirección	or direction
dame	brother —
tu mano	give me
hermano mío	your hand
que soy	I am
el carmesí	the crimson of
de tu clavel	your carnation
el viento	the wind
en busca	in search
de su raíz	of its roots
ábreme	open
las puertas	your doors
no tardes más	hurry —

no ves
que carnada
soy

para
los perros
de la oscuridad

don't
you see —
I'm bait

for
the dogs
of darkness

Izquierda

¿qué queda
de la izquierda
si el sexo
afuera se queda?

Left

what's left
of the left
if sex is
left out?

Ritual de desamor	Ritual for Unloving
el hombre	the man
arrojó	threw
una piedra	a stone
al río	into the river
la piedra	the stone
se hundió	sank
al fondo	to the bottom
como su amor	as his love
el hombre	the man
se retiró	then left
y al camino	and took
volvió	the road
más tarde	later inside
en el bolsillo	his pocket
la misma piedra	he found
se encontró	the same stone

Boricua

en el Desfile Anual Puertorriqueño de Nueva York

Nueva York
se puso
shorts
lentes oscuros

silbando
se dirigió
a la parada de
la Quinta Avenida

una bandera
puertorriqueña
le crecía
en la mano

a Nueva York
le dio calor
se quitó
la camisa

sus pechos
jóvenes
firmes
relucían

como dos
medallones
rellenos
de sol

Nueva York
llevaba
recortado
el bigote

una promesa
todavía
untada
en el pelo

y una isla
bien chévere
doblada
en la billetera

Nueva York
aplaudió
se carcajeó
gritó

tomó
cervezas
saboreó
alcapurrias

entre
los árboles
alineados
del Central Park

y lamiendo
un helado
de coco
de a peso

Nueva York
se regresó
a su esquina
de barrio

Boricua

at the Annual Puerto Rican Parade in New York

New York
put on
shorts
shades

whistling
walked to
Fifth Avenue
for the parade

a Puerto Rican
flag kept
growing
out of his hand

New York
got hot
took off
his shirt

his firm
young
pectorals
shone

like two
medallions
pumped
with sunlight

New York
showed off
his trimmed
mustache

his hair
oiled
with lots
of promise

and an island
bien chévere
folded inside
his wallet

New York
applauded
laughed
howled

drank
beers
tasted
alcapurrias

among
the lined
trees of
Central Park

and licking
his coconut
ice cream cone
for a buck

New York
went back
to his corner
in the barrio

En la boca

me queda
ay todavía
ese amargo
sabor tuyo

In My Mouth

it still lingers
oh that
bitter taste
of you

Blues del SIDA

casi todos
nuestros amigos
de San Francisco
ya se han ido

no más postales
no más llamadas
no más lágrimas
no más risas

silencio y nieblina
ahora oscurecen
nuestro antes asoleado
Distrito de la Misión

dondequiera
que ahora vamos
sólo somos un par
de extraños

AIDS Blues

almost all
our friends
in San Francisco
are gone now

no more cards
no more calls
no more tears
no more laughs

silence and fog
now darken
our once sunny
Mission District

everywhere
we go now
we're just a pair
of strangers

Pro vida	For Life
dejas	you stop
de asistir	attending
a funerales	funerals
te rehúsas	you refuse
a aceptar	to accept
la muerte	death
te pones	you start
a prender	lighting
veladoras	candles
para así	wanting to
iluminar	illuminate
las vidas	the lives
de amigos	of friends
fallecidos	gone in
en plena flor	their prime

Preguntas	Questions
después de visitar a nuestro amigo Raúl	after visiting our friend Raúl
y reírnos con él del pasado	and laughing with him about the past
en la Casa Hospicio de Santa Cruz	at the Home Hospice in Santa Cruz
donde cada día es un campo de batalla	where every day is a battleground
en su lucha diaria por la vida y contra el SIDA	in his daily fight for life and against AIDS
en coche vamos por la carretera costera	we drive back along the coast on Highway 1
ahora cada curva para nosotros es un signo más	now each curve for us is but another
de interrogación en asfalto junto al mar	asphalt question mark along the sea

¡Tlazoltéotl!

Diosa del Amor
Diosa de la Muerte
Comedora de la Suciedad
Madre de Todas las Estaciones

Madre de los Ríos
baña a tu hijo
con las aguas que brotan
de la Fuente de la Juventud

Madre de los Colibríes
sécale sus últimas lágrimas
bésale todos sus dolidos huesos
engalánalo con flores matinales

Madre de las Montañas
acarícialo con murmullos
llévatelo a tu lecho
el sueño de tu más hondo cañón

Madre de la Noche
llora con nosotros
ilumina su paso con las estrellas
de la Vía Láctea

Madre del Mar
abraza sus cenizas
hazlo coral rojo que brille
entre los grupos de peces risueñores

Madre de Todas las Estaciones
Comedora de la Suciedad
Diosa de la Muerte
Diosa del Amor

¡Tlazoltéotl!

Tlazolteotl!

Goddess of Love
Goddess of Death
Eater of Filth
Mother of All Seasons

Mother of the Rivers
cleanse your son
with waters flowing
from the Fountain of Youth

Mother of the Hummingbirds
dry off his last tears
kiss each aching bone
dress him in morning flowers

Mother of the Mountains
caress him with murmurs
take him into your bosom
the dream of your deepest canyon

Mother of the Night
weep with us
light his path with the stars
of the Milky Way

Mother of the Sea
embrace his ashes
turn him into bright red coral
amidst schools of laughing fish

Mother of All Seasons
Eater of Filth
Goddess of Death
Goddess of Love

Tlazolteotl!

Oración del desierto	Desert Prayer

montañas:
  abuelas
    olvidadas
      y recordadas
	mountains—
	  grandmothers
	    forgotten
	      and recalled

concédanos
  su aliento
    su fuerza
      su salud
	grant us
	  your breath
	    your strength
	      your health

para curarnos
  uno a otro
    —como la noche—
    las heridas
	to soothe
	  —like the night—
	    each other's
	    wounds

Afterword

Poetry as Constructing Identity: Marginality, Social Commitment, Multivalent Love, Indianness, and Feminism

Manuel de Jesús Hernández-G.

> How can we break the politics/poetics of exclusion and silence
> that have prevented the poetic expression of people like me?
> How can we empower others if we do not first empower
> ourselves? We have to empower ourselves by bringing together
> what has been disjointed, by recognizing ourselves in others, by
> accepting and celebrating who we are.
> —Francisco X. Alarcón, "The Poet as the Other"

Poet, barrio activist, university lecturer, and international traveler, Francisco X. Alarcón holds the distinction of having become, in sixteen years, a leading Chicano poet of erotic verse and social commitment, forging a human and artistic image of the Chicano/U.S. Latino. In featuring selected poems from seven previously published poetry books and one recently published collection, the anthology *From the Other Side of Night / Del otro lado de la noche: New and Selected Poems* offers the reader the opportunity to have at arm's reach the most up-to-date, balanced, and comprehensive understanding of the author's Chicano worldview. The featured poetry highlights the struggles that Chicanas and Chicanos, immigrants from Central America, Puerto Ricans, and other Latinos faced in the 1980s and 1990s, such as racism, war, exile, oppression, AIDS, homelessness, environmental pollution, and reified Aztec thought. Moreover, the title of this collection announces Alarcón's retrospective glance at the painful and conflictive journey needed to reach a self-affirming and confident Chicano subjectivity.

Although a third-generation Chicano born in Wilmington, California, Francisco X. Alarcón enjoyed the opportunity to attend primary and secondary school in both the United States and Guadalajara, Mexico. Fortunately for broader Chicano consciousness in this region, his residency and study in Mexico City inspired him to become a writer. As a doctoral student in Latin American literature at Stanford University, where he edited the journal *Vórtice* from 1978 to 1980, Alarcón won a Fulbright Fellowship, which enabled him to research Mexican literature at the prestigious Colegio de México during the academic year 1982–83. While residing in Mexico City, he met the award-winning Mexican poet Elías Nandino, who became his role model and soul mate.[1]

Upon his return from Mexico, Alarcón began his career both as a teacher and a poet. In addition to holding a lecturer position in the Spanish for Spanish-Speakers Program at both the University of California at Santa Cruz (1985–92) and the University of California at Davis (1992–present), he has published several poetry collections and four children's books, in the process garnering several noteworthy literary awards for his work (the American Book Award, the National Parenting Publications Book Award, the Carlos Pellicer–Robert Frost Poetry Honor Award, the Pura Belpré Honor Award). He also coedited the best Spanish textbook available for bilingual speakers, *Mundo 21,* in the market. In addition, he has given several keynote speeches at baccalaureates and has been a resident poet at various colleges and universities.

Beginning with *Tattoos* (1985), which earned him the 1981 Primer Premio Latinoamericano de Poesía–Rubén Darío, Alarcón has up to this point published ten poetry books for adults. The three most important ones in his writing career are *Body in Flames / Cuerpo en llamas* (1990), *De amor oscuro / Of Dark Love* (1991), and *Snake Poems: An Aztec Invocation* (1992). To this list of important works we should add the current volume, which is the most comprehensive collection of his work to date. As a unit, the first three texts feature the evolution of a unified erotic and activist vision. However, Alarcón underwent several artistic changes from 1981 to 1989 before reaching such a worldview. In retrospect, *Ya vas, carnal* (1989) stands as a transitional work. Featuring fifteen poems by Alarcón and a set each by the poets Rodrigo Reyes and Juan Pablo Gutiérrez, the collection is the first publicly declared gay literary work published and distributed within the Chicano/U.S. Latino literary circuit; it contains direct and highly homoerotic images. The four collections *Quake Poems* (1989), *Loma Prieta* (1990), *Poemas zurdos* (1992), and *No Golden Gate for Us* (1993) offer primarily situational or feature poems from previously published poetry books by the author. For example, prepared in Spanish for the Mexican reader, *Poemas zurdos* is a mini-anthology of poems taken from *Tattoos, Ya vas, carnal, Loma Prieta, Body in Flames,* and *No Golden Gate for Us.* And finally, in the more recent *Sonnets to Madness and Other Misfortunes / Sonetos a la locura y otras penas* (2001), Alarcón again revives the sonnet form to speak to a new generation.

A UNIFIED EROTIC AND ACTIVIST VISION: *BODY IN FLAMES, DE AMOR OSCURO, SNAKE POEMS*

In an introductory poem and a closing poem framing four thematic sections, *Body in Flames* presents a unified Chicano poetic voice, one that is both communal and activist. (This same structure, by the way, frames the selected poems included in the current anthology.) To achieve such a balance in *Body in Flames,* Alarcón used, with some revision, several poems from *Tattoos* and *Ya vas, carnal.* In this way, *Body in Flames* forms part of an already established social continuum whose struggles remain identity, marginality, and regeneration. The new poems in that volume, "El otro día me encontré a García Lorca / The Other Day I Ran into García Lorca," "El amor no existe / Love Doesn't Exist," and "Mi pelo / My Hair" reintroduce the homoerotic dimension. Building on the then-recent rediscovery and publication of gay poetry by Federico García Lorca (1898–1936), "El otro día me encontré a García Lorca" features an Andalusian poet who plants an intimate kiss on the mouth of the Chicano poetic I. In such an image, openness rules the gay poetic voice. "Mi pelo" reclaims tenderness and playfulness as deep-seated in a gay relationship, with the image of gray hair on the head of the poetic I symbolizing longevity. In "El amor no existe," the image of the lovers' shadows embracing on a café window empties the semantic content of the title. The third section of *Body in Flames* expands the homoerotic vision, claiming that gay love originates in the unsaid or the senses. Using hyperbolic metaphors where geography sites equal human body parts (thighs, the chest, the mouth, tongue), the opening poem of this section, "Todo es un cuerpo inmenso / Everything Is an Immense Body," illustrates this new sensuality.

In *Body in Flames,* the activist dimension experiences equal development, section by section. Taken from *Tattoos,* the poem "I Used to Be Much Much Darker" marks the social continuum in Alarcón's activist voice. The first section of *Body in Flames* details Chicano childhood in California from the 1960s to the 1970s: a working-class neighborhood, racism, oral tales, graffiti, miseducation, the writer's marginality, and barrio allegiance. In expanding the subject's historical vision, the second section examines the struggles of the 1980s in the Chicano/U.S. Latino community: women's rights, opposition to torture in Central America, revindication of gay love, and self-defense. The poetic I sees in matriarchy a source of freedom and struggle. For example, in opposition to male oppression of mother, daughter, and wife as featured in the verses of "Cuarto oscuro / Dark Room," the poem "Una pequeña gran victoria / A Small but Fateful Victory" features a rebellious and triumphant sister and mother. As an expression of feminism, matriarchy becomes a recurring ideologeme in Alarcón's poetry. Concomitantly, such a position means the rejection of patriarchy; in the poem "Mi padre / My Father," the poetic I feels like a stranger before his father but soon realizes that both of them reject "that nightmare / called / macho."

The unified homoerotic and activist dimension in *Body in Flames* provided Alarcón with the ability to focus on one or the other with equal mastery in his next two collections: *De amor oscuro / Of Dark Love* and *Snake Poems*. Whereas *Snake Poems* examines Chicanos both historically and globally, *De amor oscuro* immortalizes Chicano love, becoming the first collection in Mexican American poetry wholly dedicated to the emotion of love. Two specific poems from *Body in Flames,* "Anatomía presagiosa / Prophetic Anatomy" and "El otro día me encontré a García Lorca / The Other Day I Ran into García Lorca," serve as the inspiration and sensual parameters for *De amor oscuro.* "Anatomía presagiosa" establishes these sensual parameters in two ways: it privileges the senses as the source of love and places emphasis on the lover's body, in particular the upper extremities and their respective motion. After the introductory sonnet in *De amor oscuro* defines Chicano love as multivalent, sonnets two to seven celebrate its sensual expression in the lover: the arms, the voice, the hands, the shoulders, the sleeping body, and the legs. From a metaliterary level, these seven sonnets and number eight express the problem of the existence of Chicano love. The remaining six sonnets offer the solution: not its suppression, but its acceptance by the general community. Unlike the free, competitive, and intensive sensuality in John Rechy's novel *Numbers* (1967),[2] the expression of love in *De amor oscuro* is mythic, innocent, religious, and mystical. Allegorized by Greco-Roman and Christian imagery, this conception of love stands as unique in Chicano poetry and letters.

Antipodally to *De amor oscuro,* the volume *Snake Poems: An Aztec Invocation* immerses the poetic I in the activist dimension. Except for an Aztec invocation speaking for lovers, this collection distances itself from erotic verse. Instead, the poetic I retraces historically the Chicano social condition to Mexico's colonial period under Spain and examines the people's present standing in the United States.[3] Far from being an apocryphal text, *Snake Poems* intertwines, particularly in the six middle sections, Aztec invocations with a series of poems on the current Chicano condition, calling attention to the pressing social agenda. As a rule, each original poem addresses a particular issue: section 1 includes the poem "Midnight Water Song," which calls forth the spirits of the desert, and it ends with an invocation for spiritual rebirth in the poem "Ololiuhqui." "Chicome-Xochitl / Seven Flower," in section 2, praises deer in the wilderness; "Ode to Tomatoes," in section 3, celebrates the contribution of this Mesoamerican fruit to the world's diet; "Potent Seeds," in section 4, champions corn; "Tonantzin" and "Cihuacoatl," in section 6, privilege female freedom and rebellion; and "Working Hands," also in section 6, identifies Chicano workers as the democratic voice of the community.[4] The sections entitled "Tahui" and "New Day" feature all original poems by Alarcón and frame the six sections noted above, which are made up of Aztec invocations. This presentation marks the inversion of suppressed Aztec thought as necessary to the process of understanding colonization and foregrounds Chicano subordination in the United States, which conscious struggle can change.

Several themes in Alarcón's previous work code the return of the poetic I to its activist dimension. As a structuring ideologeme, matriarchy undergoes considerable expansion in *Snake Poems*. Placed in the section entitled "Healers," the poems "Matriarch" and "Tonantzin" mark the links between the figure of the grandmother in *Body in Flames* and Tonantzin, Our Mother. The figure of the matriarch has evolved to the level of goddess, a symbolically omnipotent yet liberating leader. Moreover, as the Virgin of Guadalupe, Tonantzin not only leads other goddesses—such as Coatlicue, Chalchiuhcueye, and Citlalcueye— but also holds the banners of hope and rebellion for the Chicano people in their continued subordination. This matriarchal dimension has its base outside *Snake Poems*. In joining Chicano feminists, Alarcón sees the revindication of matriarchy as a necessary step in the formation of a nonsexist society.

FROM THE OTHER SIDE OF NIGHT: RETURN TO A LONG-STANDING POETIC PROJECT

The publication of this current anthology represents Alarcón's return to his long-standing poetic project. With regard to content, structure, and significance, this latest collection is similar to *Body in Flames,* yet more thorough because it includes selections from *Loma Prieta* and *No Golden Gate for Us* as well as from more recent work. However, as its title implies, the reader now hears an experienced, self-conscious, and mature Chicano voice, one that recognizes that the Chicano subject has claimed some space in society for Chicanos/U.S. Latinos. The volume strongly reaffirms both Alarcón's past work and its activist and loving voice.

The section "Sonnets to Madness and Other Misfortunes / Sonetos a la locura y otras penas" features eight of twenty-four poems from the recently published poetry book of the same title. The introductory poem, "Nuevo día / New Day," links this section to Alarcón's first published poetry collection, *Tattoos*, where the poem carried the title "Poet in prison / Mundo"; however, the semantic content of the poem, laden with oppression, is inverted as the poetic I now speaks about a spontaneous and open expression of Chicano/Latino love in four of the sonnets: "Abrazarte quisiera, viento mío / I want to embrace you, dear wind," "Tus ojos me enseñan de nuevo a ver / Your eyes show me how to see again," "Entonces las horas eran tan largas / Back then hours were so long," and "Escúchame como aquel eco perdido / Listen to me like that echo lost." In fact, the fourth poem turns out to be a carpe diem calling for the maximum enjoyment of physical love, as illustrated in its imagery based on nature.

The sonnet "Y dije adiós como quien muerde el aire / And I said good-bye as if biting the air" examines a Chicano's difficult and painful relationship with his parents and should be read in connection to the poem "Mi padre / My Father" from *Body in Flames*. Finally, the last two sonnets included in *From the Other Side of the Night*, "Las palabras son llaves enmohecidas / Words are rusted keys" and "Tras este lenguaje hay otro más antiguo / Beneath this language, there's another," return to a continuing and always urgent reexamination of language from the perspective of the Chicano poetic subject.

In addition to giving the title to this poetry anthology, the section "From the Other Side of Night / Del otro lado de la noche" features a mature Chicano gay subject who has ceased to feel overpowered by society, has earned some victories, and is intimately aware of the complexities of the human condition. The title poem foregrounds fear and self-affirmation as structuring ideologemes in this specific section and in the anthology as a whole. Silence and liminality do remain today as problems for Chicanos/U.S. Latinos: "we are yet / to be / appear / exist"; on the other hand, as human beings, these people are bountiful and limitless: "here / nobody knows / nor will know / of the sea / we carry / within us / of the fire / we ignite / with our bodies / from / the other side / of night." In this anthology, the night ceases to be an oppressive and anonymous space, pathological at times, as previously established by the poem "Prófugo / Fugitive" from *Ya vas, carnal* and in subsequent poetry collections *(Body in Flames, Poemas zurdos).* Such symbolism linked to the night is also present in various poems found in other collections — for example, the poem "Silence," which first appeared in *Snake Poems* and was reprinted in *No Golden Gate for Us.* Instead, the night has now evolved into a contemplative space from where a Chicano subject reflects on his life in light of an evolutionary process: identity, marginality, struggle, and regeneration.

Five of fourteen new poems in *From the Other Side of Night,* "Para nosotros / For Us," "Encuentro / Encounter," "Afuera / Out," "Plegaria de amor / Love Plea," and "Izquierda / Left," celebrate love as a dynamic and liberating force. However, the poems "Ritual del desamor / Ritual for Unloving" and "En la boca / In My Mouth" counterbalance with illustrations of bad yet unforgettable relationships. In line with Alarcón's socially committed verse, the poems "Blues del SIDA / AIDS Blues," "Pro vida / For Life," "Preguntas / Questions," "¡Tlazotéotl! / Tlazoteotl!" and "Oración del desierto / Desert Prayer" question the heavy death toll from AIDS among friends and acquaintances. In a desperate yet resourceful rebellion, the poetic I involves itself in struggle by performing traditional Catholic ritual such as lighting a veladora or candle in "Pro vida / For Life" and by reciting mythic Aztec incantation in "¡Tlazotéotl! / Tlazoteotl!" Again, this grief is counterbalanced by the celebration of life in the poem "Boricua," which extols Neoyorican culture in its description of the annual Puerto Rican Parade in New York.

MASTER OF CHICANO
MINIMALIST VERSE AND POEM

Alarcón is the master of both minimalist verse and the minimalist poem in Chicano poetry. Notwithstanding, he uses with equal skill in his writing such high forms as the sonnet and the long poem. As seen in *Tattoos,* Alarcón initiated his writing career using minimalist verse (from one to four syllables) and the minimalist poem (one to two stanzas). All but four poems in this very first collection are minimalist in structure. Although limited in verse length, such minimalist writing serves as the formal rhetorical base in *Ya vas, carnal, Loma Prieta, Body in Flames, Snake Poems,* and *No Golden Gate for Us.* In fact, Alarcón parted with minimalist verse, stanza, and poem only when he sat down to write the collection *De amor oscuro,* where he accepted the challenge of the sonnet form in Spanish.

However, Alarcón's sonnet writing has evolved into a hybrid form. He does keep the required fourteen hendecasyllable lines—the two quatrains with the problem and the two tercets with the resolution—but he does not follow any set scheme in rhyming the fourteen lines. His hybrid sonnet form rises to an even higher level of complexity in *Sonnets to Madness and Other Misfortunes.* Some sonnets shift the statement of the problem from the quatrains to the tercets, and some initiate the resolution in the first two stanzas—for example, "Entonces las horas eran tan largas / Back then hours were so long." For his imagery, Alarcón draws, like the Chilean poet Pablo Neruda, from plants, geography, and stars. Thus, images based on nature and the cosmos predominate in configuring the lover in *Sonnets to Madness* as well as in *De amor oscuro* and in the incantations in *Snake Poems.* In fact, images based on nature mark the lovers present in all of the poetry books Alarcón has published to date.

ALARCÓN'S SIGNIFICANCE: AN EVOLVING WORLDVIEW

Through his community activism, his consistent dedication to the Chicano/U.S. Latino literary circuit, and the creative work for which he has received literary awards and honors from both the Latino community and mainstream America, Francisco X. Alarcón has committed a prodigious act. He has molded in sequence (1) a significant contribution to literature, which includes a dual erotic and social vision; (2) an authentic image of the Chicano based on openness about sexual and cultural preference; (3) a poetic discourse that features community struggles from the 1970s to the new millennium; (4) a vanguard role in the establishment of a creative space available to Chicanos/U. S. Latinos; and (5) an appropriation of model artistic forms as well as old and new linguistic signs. In a noteworthy achievement comparable to the last edition of Walt Whitman's *Leaves of Grass,* the present anthology offers the reader the opportunity to know and understand the evolving worldview of a Chicano/U.S. Latino poetic voice.

1. See Francisco X. Alarcón, "The Poet as the Other," in *Chicano/Latino Homoerotic Identities,* edited by David William Foster (New York: Garland, 1999), 161.

2. John Rechy, *Numbers,* rev. ed. (New York: Grove Press, 1984).

3. According to the critic Alfred Arteaga, *Snake Poems* "is an encounter with another text completed in 1629 by one Hernando Ruiz de Alarcón, a Catholic priest from Atenango, a small town in the present State of Guerrero, Mexico" ("Before These Poems, and After," in *Snake Poems: An Aztec Invocation,* by Francisco X. Alarcón [San Francisco: Chronicle Books, 1992], ix). As Arteaga sees it, whereas Ruiz de Alarcón wrote *Tratado de las supersticiones y costumbres gentílicas que hoy viven entre los indios naturales desta Nueva España* (Treatise on the Superstitions and Heathen Customs That Today Live among the Indians Native to This New Spain) "to expose heathen practice among the Indians and extend the repressive practice of the Spanish Inquisition in Mexico," Francisco X. Alarcón has captured in *Snake Poems* "the spirit of the Indian Informants, a sense of Native culture alive despite the best efforts to misread and suppress it" ("Before These Poems," ix, x). For further information on the intertextuality and ideological difference between *Snake Poems* and *Tratado de las supersticiones,* see Arteaga, "Before These Poems, and After"; Hernando Ruiz de Alarcón, "Tratado de las supersticiones y costumbres gentílicas que hoy viven entre los indios naturales desta Nueva España," in *El alma encantada: Anales del Museo Nacional de México. Presentación de Fernando Benítez,* edited by Pedro Ponce et al. (Mexico City: Instituto Nacional Indigenista / Fondo de Cultura Económica, 1987), 123–224 (facsimile edition of *Anales del Museo Nacional de México,* vol. 6 [1892]); and Hernando Ruiz de Alarcón, *Treatise on the Heathen Superstitions That Today Live among the Indians Native to this New Spain, 1629,* edited and translated by J. Richard and Ross Hassig (Norman: University of Oklahoma Press, 1984).

4. In section 6 of *Snake Poems,* the poem "In Ixtli In Yollotl / Face and Heart" attributes true wisdom to the common people involved in the struggle for social justice.

Glossary

All words are derived from Nahuatl if not otherwise noted.

alcapurria: Spanish word for a tasty traditional Puerto Rican snack made of fried dough.

amor zurdo: Spanish for "left-handed love."

atole: A thick drink or gruel made of cornmeal of various consistencies and flavors; derived from *atolli,* which is formed by *atl,* "water," and *tlaolli,* "corn."

Aztec: Nahuatl-speaking group that migrated south from Aztlán ("Place of Herons"), which many contemporary Chicanos identify as their U.S. Southwest homeland and which is the origin of the word *Aztec;* this group was also known as the *Mexica* (pronounced "Meshica"), from which the words *Mexicano* and *Chicano* are derived. In 1325, the Aztecs founded Tenochtitlán on a small island in Lake Texcoco, where an eagle was devouring a serpent; they aggressively conquered the surrounding Indian groups and were themselves vanquished by new diseases and a combined Indian-Spanish army led by Hernán Cortés in 1521.

bien chévere: Spanish colloquial expression that corresponds to "real cool."

Boricua: Term derived from *Borinquen,* the original Taíno name for the Island of Puerto Rico; it is used as synonymous to *Puerto Rican,* both on the island and in the continental United States.

carnal: In Spanish, this word literally means "fleshy, carnal"; Chicanos use it to mean "brother" or "intimate friend"; *carnalito, carnalita* are the Spanish diminutive forms that connote affection.

Centeotl: Ear-of-Corn-God, from *centli,* "dried ear of corn," and *teotl,* "god"; Ruiz de Alarcón translated it as "the only god," a misinterpretation because he takes *cen-* to mean "one."

Cenzontle: Derived by apocope from *centzontlatolltototl,* "bird of four hundred songs or voices," which is from *centzontli,* "four hundred," *tlatolli,* "word," and *tototl,* "bird"; a tropical songbird very much appreciated for its great singing versatility.

Chalchiuhcueye: Jade-Skirt-Owner, from *chalchihuitl,* "jade," *cueitl,* "skirt," *ye,* "who owns"; Goddess of the Water.

Chichimec: Term for the nomadic and hunting tribes arriving to Mesoamerica after the Toltecs in the twelfth century; name of the barbaric tribes from the north; some have identified this word to mean "Dog People."

Chicome-Xochitl: Seven Flower, from *chicome,* "seven" (*chic-ome,* "five plus two"), and *xochitl,* "flower"; a calendrical name; also a ritual name for the male deer.

Cihuacoatl: Snake Woman, from *cihuatl,* "woman," and *coatl,* "snake"; known as La Llorona in Mexico and the U.S. Southwest.

Cipactonal: Alligator-Spirit, from *cipactli,* "alligator," and *tonal,* "spirit." *Cipactli* is the glyph of the first day in the Mesoamerican twenty-day month, symbolizing the first animal able to move from the sea to dry land. She is the first woman in the Mesoamerican primordial couple; in Nahuatl mythology, she is credited together with her spouse, Oxomoco, for originating the divinatory arts.

Citlalcueye: Star-Skirt-Owner, from *citlalin,* "star," *cueitl,* "skirt," and *ye,* "who owns"; Nahuatl name for the Milky Way.

Coatlicue: Snake-Skirted-One, from *coatl,* "snake," and *icue,* "it is her skirt"; Fertility Goddess.

corazón: Spanish for "heart."

flor: Spanish for "flower"; the title of the poem "Las flores son nuestras armas" is Spanish for "Flowers Are Our Weapons."

Guadalupe: Patron saint of Mexico, a syncretic religious figure that includes Mesoamerican, Christian, and Arabic elements. According to tradition, she appeared and spoke in Nahuatl to native Juan

Diego in Tepeyac, where Tonantzin, "Our Mother Goddess," was worshiped; she has been espoused by several social movements and causes both in Mexico and the Southwest; for example, she was on the first Mexican flag of Father Miguel Hidalgo's native army fighting for independence from Spain in 1810 and on the banner of the mestizo popular armies of Emiliano Zapata in the Mexican Revolution of 1910; she also appeared in California amidst picket signs in the 1965 Delano grape strike organized by Chicano union leader César Chávez.

hamaca: Spanish word derived from a Taíno term; "hammock."

Huehueh: Old Man, a metaphor for fire. It is also another name for Oxomoco; in classical times, Huehueteotl—from *huehuetl,* "old man" and *teotl,* "god"—was the name of the God of Fire, one of the oldest deities in Mesoamerica.

in ixtli in yollotl: "Face and heart," figurative phrase for truth and sincerity, formed by setting together *ixtli,* "face," and *yollotl,* "heart."

in xochitl in cuicatl: "Flower and song," figurative phrase for poetry, formed by setting together *xochitl,* "flower," and *cuicatl,* "song." Chicanos have used the Spanish equivalent, *floricanto,* to name the poetry and cultural festivals in their communities since the late 1960s.

La Llorona: Spanish for "Crying Woman," a mythical woman who cries up and down looking for her lost children around water sources, very much alive in folk legends throughout Mexico and the U.S. Southwest; derived from the Aztec legend of Cihuacoatl, Snake Woman.

maíz: Spanish word derived from the Taíno name for corn; the Nahuatl equivalent is *tlaolli,* "dried, shelled corn," or *centli,* "dried, unshelled corn."

Matl: The Hand; in his 1629 *Tratado,* Ruiz de Alarcón uses it as another name for Quetzalcoatl.

mestizo: Spanish word that identifies a person of mixed racial/ethnic background; it does not have the negative connotations of its English equivalents "half-breed" or "half-caste"; Latinos both in Latin America and in the United States have increasingly accepted it as a term of self-identity.

mijito: Spanish colloquial apocope of *mi hijito,* "my little son" or "my dearest son."

Moquequeloatzin: The-One-Who-Makes-Fun-of-Himself, another name for Tezcatlipoca.

nahual: Derived from *nahualli,* "sorcerer" or "magician"; in the *Tratado,* it signifies a sorcerer who supposedly is able to transform himself or herself into an animal or the animal that is the alter ego, the *tonal,* or the guardian spirit that accompanies a person throughout his or her life.

Nahualteuctli: Nahualli-Lord, enchanter, from *nahualli,* "sorcerer," and *teuctli,* "lord."

Nahuatl: Language from the Uto-Aztecan linguistic family that extended from the U.S. Southwest, Mexico, and Central America; spoken by the Toltecs, Aztecs, Pipiles, and many other native groups. Hundreds of Spanish and English words are derived from Nahuatl; the term comes from the verb *nahuati,* "to speak clearly."

Nana: Familiar term for "mother," from the endearment *nanatzin,* "little mother."

niño barrigón: Spanish for "big belly boy."

Nomatca nehuatl: "I myself," magical formula for personal empowerment found in most Nahuatl spells in the *Tratado;* Ruiz de Alarcón translates it as a phrase, "I myself in person" or "I in person"; linguists J. Richard Andrews and Ross Hassing translate it as a sentence with *nehuatl,* "I am the one" or "it is I," and with *nomatca* as an adverbial modifier, "in person."

Olmec: Mother culture of the Mesoamerican civilization; it refers to people "from the land of rubber."

Ololiuhqui: Name for medicinal herb whose seeds are round, from *ololihui,* "round like a ball"; it is used as an oracle in the *Tratado.* Also known as *coaxiuth,* "snake herb," it causes hallucinations.

Oxomoco: Turpentine Ointment–Two-Pine Torches, compound name derived from *oxitl,* "turpentine ointment," *ome,* "two," and *ocotl,* "pine torches"; *ocote* is the stick of pine kindling. He is the first man in the Mesoamerican primordial couple; in Nahuatl mythology, he is credited, together with his spouse, Cipactonal, for originating the divinatory arts. Oxomoco is also known as Huehueh, "Old Man," which at times is used as a metaphor for fire.

patria: Spanish for "fatherland" or "homeland."

peyote: Name of diverse kinds of cactaceous plants used for medicinal and spiritual purposes, its fruit or "button" has hallucinogenic properties; from *peyotl,* "a thing that glimmers, glows"; it is used as the main sacrament of the Native American Church, a Pan-Indian religious or spiritual movement that has extended throughout native groups in North America.

Quetzalcoatl: Plumed Serpent, god and cultural hero of a central myth and historic legend in Mexico and Yucatán, where he was known by the Mayan name Kukulcan; *quetzalcoatl* is a compound noun derived from *quetzalli,* "precious feather," and *coatl,* "snake"; he is identified with Ehecatl, the God of Wind, and with the planet Venus; as a Toltec cultural hero, Ce-Acatl Topiltzin Quetzalcoatl (Ce-Acatl, "1 Reed," is his calendrical name, whereas Topiltzin is a compound name formed by the prefix *to-,* "our," and *piltzin,* "lord"), he promised to return after being defeated by the priests of the new cult of Tezcatlipoca. Hernán Cortés was identified with this deity when he first appeared on the shores of the Aztec Empire in 1519, the year Ce-Acatl, which was the date prophesied for the return of Lord Quetzalcoatl.

tenexiete: Lime tobacco, from *tenextli,* "lime" (which is itself a compound noun formed by *tetl,* "stone," and *nextli,* "ash"), and *iyetl,* "tobacco"; it is ground *piciete* mixed with lime.

Tezcatlipoca: Smoking Mirror, the god of the sorcerers, also known as Yaotl, "the Warrior," and Telpochtli, "the Eternally Young"; originally, he symbolized the night sky, thus his name, Smoking Mirror, from *tezcatl,* "mirror," and *ipoca,* "it emits smoke." A Mesoamerican legend tells how he, jealous of wise Quetzalcoatl, lured the good king into drunkenness and incest with his sister, Xochiquetzal, and then he showed Quetzalcoatl his face in the "mirror that smokes," whereupon Quetzalcoatl, penitent for his guilt, migrated south and set to sea on a raft of rattlesnakes with the promise that he would return in the year Ce-Acatl ("1 Reed"), which was the year Hernán Cortés and his fleet arrived.

Tlalteuctli: Lord of the Land, compound noun formed by *tlalli,* "land," and *teuctli,* "lord"; in the *Tratado,* Ruiz de Alarcón identifies this deity as Goddess of the Earth.

Tlamacazqui: Spirit, priest; it literally means "one who will give something"; in the *Tratado,* it is the term for any power entity.

Tlazolteotl: Love Goddess, from *tlazotli,* "beloved," and *teotl,* "god, goddess."

Tlazopilli: Beloved Prince, Beloved Princess, a ritual name for corn; from *tlazotli,* "precious, beloved thing," and *pilli,* "nobleman, noblewoman."

Toltec: Nahuatl-speaking group whose capital was Tollan; for later native peoples in Mesoamerica, *toltecatl* signified "artist."

Tonacacihuatl: Lady of Our Flesh, compound noun formed by the prefix *to-,* "our," *nacatl,* "flesh," "sustenance," and *cihuatl,* "woman"; another name for Xochiquetzal, the Love Goddess; it is also used in the *Tratado* as a ritual name for corn.

tonal: Soul, spirit, from the Nahuatl word *tonalli,* "sunlike," which is derived from the verb *tona,* "to shine, to be sunny, to be warm."

Tonalamatl: Book or codex of days or destinies, compound name formed by *tonal,* "day," "destiny," and also "spirit," and *amatl,* "bark paper"; it was a book used for divination and as an astrological almanac.

Tonantzin: Our Mother, compound noun formed by the prefix *to-,* "our," and *nantli,* "mother," together with the suffix *-tzin,* which indicates endearment and respect; Nahuatl name for the Virgen de Guadalupe, the patron saint of Mexico; in classical times, it was another name for Centeotl, the Corn Deity.

Tonatiuh: Sun God, the name of the Fifth Sun in the Nahuatl creation myth.

Xochiquetzal: Precious Flower, Love Goddess, from *xochitl,* "flower," and *quetzal,* "precious plume"; goddess of flowers, arts, and crafts; also known as Tonacacihuatl and Chalchiuhcueye.

xochitl: Flower, also the last day of the Mesoamerican twenty-day month.

Yaotl: The Warrior, another name for Tezcatlipoca.

Critical Works

Alarcón, Francisco X. "Dialéctica del amor / Dialectics of Love: Words
of Warning." In *Virgins, Guerrillas, and Locas: Gay Latinos Writing
about Love,* edited by Jaime Cortez, 105–17. San Francisco: Cleis
Press, 1999.

——. "The Poet as the Other." In *Chicano/Latino Homoerotic
Identities,* edited by David William Foster, 159–74. New York:
Garland Publishing, 1999.

——. "Reclaiming Ourselves, Reclaiming America." In *Without
Discovery: A Native Response to Columbus,* edited by Ray González,
29–38. Seattle: Broken Moon Press, 1992.

Arteaga, Alfred. "Before These Poems, and After." In *Snake Poems:
An Aztec Invocation,* by Francisco X. Alarcón, ix–xi. San Francisco:
Chronicle Books, 1992.

——. *Chicano Poetics: Heterotexts and Hybridities.* New York:
Cambridge University Press, 1997.

Ausbel, Kenny. "Francisco X. Alarcón Rediscovers the Americas." In
Restoring the Earth: Visionary Solutions from the Bioneers, 71–84.
Tiburon, Calif.: H. J. Kramer, 1997.

Bell, Dan. "Chants Encounter: Francisco X. Alarcón's Aztec Way of
Knowledge." *Village Voice* (October 27, 1992): 73–74.

Corraine, Diego. "Poesias dae 'Cuerpo en llamas': Su poeta e su populu
de sos tzicanos." In *Andelas: Bidas, Paristorias, Contos, Poesias 1,*
79–94. Nouro, Sardinia: Papiros, 1994.

Eng, Karen. "*Snake Poems: An Aztec Invocation* by Francisco X. Alarcón." *Shaman's Drum* (summer 1992): 67–68.

Evans, Terri. "Poet's Mystic Roots." *Suttertown News* (Santa Cruz, Calif.), April 15–22, 1993, 6–7.

Foster, David William. "The Poetry of Francisco X. Alarcón: The Queer Project of Poetry." In *Chicano/Latino Homoerotic Identities,* edited by David William Foster, 175–95. New York: Garland Publishing, 1999.

González, Marcial. "The Poetry of Francisco X. Alarcón: Identifying the Chicano Persona." *Bilingual Review* 19, no. 2 (May–August 1994): 179–87.

Griffin, Noel, and Baile Átha Cliath. "Introduction / Réamhrá." In *Colainn ar Bharr Lasrach,* translated by Gabriel Rosenstock, 11–23. Indreabhán, Conamara, Ireland: Cló Iar-Chonnachta, 1992.

Hartley, George. "Hegemony and Identity: The Chicano Hybrid in Francisco X. Alarcón's Snake Poems." *Studies in Twentieth Century Literature* 25, no. 1 (Winter 2001): 281–305.

Hernández-G., Manuel de Jesús. "Alarcón, Franciso X. (United States; 1954)." In *Latin American Writers on Gay and Lesbian Themes: A Bio-critical Sourcebook,* edited by David William Foster, 7–13. Westport, Conn.: Greenwood Press, 1994.

———. "Building a Research Agenda on U.S. Latino Lesbigay Literature and Cultural Production: Texts, Writers, Performance, and Critics." In *Chicano/Latino Homoerotic Identities,* edited by David William Foster, 287–325. New York: Garland Publishing, 1999.

Holder, Kathleen. "From the Bellybutton from the Heart." *UC Davis Magazine* 17, no. 4 (summer 2000): 20–23.

Kessler, Stephen. "Consoling the Flowers." *Poetry Flash: A Poetry Review and Literary Calendar for the West* 233 (August 1992): 1, 4–5, and 8.

Leone, Robert. "Palabras Heridas: An Interview with Francisco X. Alarcón." *Lector* 5, no. 1 (summer 1985): 18–21.

Lundgren, Arne. "Mexikaner i USA." In *Cuerpo en llamas / Kropp i lågor,* by Francisco X. Alarcón, translated by Utta Nättarqvist-Sawa, 7–17. Lysekil, Sweden: Fabians Förlag. 1991.

Maxwell, Alberto, and Miguel Pérez. "Dos artistas en la calle: Arte en tránsito." *Horizontes Culturales* (suplemento, San Francisco), agosto 20, 1993, 12–13.

Morrow, Steve. "The Poetry and the Lessons of the Aztec." *The New Mexican* (Santa Fe, New Mexico), October 25, 1992, E1–2.

Muñoz, Elías Miguel. "Corpus of Words and Flesh: *Body in Flames / Cuerpo en llamas*." *Bilingual Review* 16, nos. 2–3 (1991): 235–40.

Nizalowski, John. "A Bilingual Poet Who Explodes Myths." *The New Mexican* (Santa Fe, New Mexico), March 30, 1990, 27 and 30.

Pérez-Torres, Rafael. *Movements in Chicano Poetry: Against Myths, against Margins.* New York: Cambridge University Press, 1997.

Quitner, Jeremy. "Dreamer's World." *Bay Area Reporter: Arts and Entertainment* 22, no. 22 (May 28, 1992): 29 and 38–40.

Review of *Colainn ar Bharr Lasrach / Cuerpo en llamas*, by Francisco X. Alarcón. *Books Ireland* (April 1992): 86.

Rodríguez del Pino, Salvador. "Francisco X. Alarcón." In *Chicano Writers: Second Series,* edited by Francisco Lomelí and Carl R. Shirley, 3–7. Detroit: Gale Research, 1992.

Scambray, Kara. "Alarcón Explores Many Facets of Life." *California Aggie* (Davis, Calif.), November 30, 1992, front and back pages.

Sherman, Ann Elliot. Book Review: "*No Golden Gate for Us —* Homelands: The Poet Inside." *Metro* (February 18–24, 1993): n.p.

Underwood, Leticia Iliana. "Confluencia de textos y voces en la poesía de Francisco X. Alarcón: *Poemas serpiente: una invocación azteca.*" *Explicación de Textos Literarios* 26, no. 2 (1997–98): 20–43.

Collections of poetry by Francisco X. Alarcón

1985   *Tattoos* (Oakland, California: Nomad Press)

1989   *Quake Poems* (Santa Cruz, Calif.: We Press)
Ya vas, carnal (San Francisco: Humanizarte Publications)

1990   *Body in Flames / Cuerpo en llamas,* translated by Francisco
Aragón (San Francisco: Chronicle Books)
Loma Prieta (Santa Cruz, Calif.: We Press)

1991   *De amor oscuro / Of Dark Love,* translated by Francisco Aragón
(Santa Cruz, Calif.: Moving Parts Press)
Cuerpo en llamas / Kropp i Lågor, translated by Ulla Nätterqvist-
Sawa (Lysekil, Sweden: Fabians Förlag)

1992   *Cuerpo en llamas / Collainn ar bharr lasrach,* translated by Gabriel
Rosenstock (Indreabhán, Ireland: Cló Iar-Connachta Teo)
De amor oscuro / Vin an ngrá dorcha, translated by Gabriel
Rosenstock (Indreabhán, Ireland: Cló Iar-Connachta Teo)
Poemas zurdos (Mexico City: Editorial Factor)
Snake Poems: An Aztec Invocation (San Francisco: Chronicle
Books)

1993   *No Golden Gate for Us* (Tesuque, N.Mex.: Pennywhistle Press)

1997   *Laughing Tomatoes and Other Spring Poems / Jitomates risueños y
otros poemas de primavera* (San Francisco: Children's Book Press)

1998   *From the Bellybutton of the Moon and Other Summer Poems /
Del ombligo de la luna y otros poemas de verano* (San Francisco:
Children's Book Press)

1999   *Angels Ride Bikes and Other Fall Poems / Los ángeles andan en
bicicleta y otros poemas de otoño* (San Francisco: Children's Book
Press)

2001   *Sonnets to Madness and Other Misfortunes / Sonetos a la locura y
otras penas* (Berkeley: Creative Arts Book Company)
*Iguanas in the Snow and Other Winter Poems / Iguanas en la nieve
y otros poemas de invierno* (San Francisco: Children's Book Press)

About the Author

FRANCISCO X. ALARCÓN, Chicano poet and educator, was born in Los Angeles, California, in 1954, grew up Guadalajara, Mexico, and is the author of ten volumes of poetry, including *Body in Flames / Cuerpo en llamas* (Chronicle Books, 1990), *De amor oscuro / Of Dark Love* (Moving Parts Press, 1991 and 2001), *Snake Poems: An Aztec Invocation* (Chronicle Books, 1992), *No Golden Gate for Us* (Pennywhistle Press, 1993), and *Sonnets to Madness and Other Misfortunes / Sonetos a la locura y otras penas* (Creative Arts Book Company, 2001). Two of his books of bilingual poetry for children, *Laughing Tomatoes and Other Spring Poems* (Children's Book Press, 1997) and *From the Bellybutton of the Moon and Other Summer Poems* (Children's Book Press, 1998) won the Pura Belpré Honor Award by the American Library Association in 1998 and 2000. He has published two other collections of bilingual poetry for children, *Angels Ride Bikes and Other Fall Poems* (Children's Book Press, 1999) and *Iguanas in the Snow and Other Winter Poems* (Children's Book Press, 2001). He has been a recipient of the Danforth and Fulbright Fellowships, and has been awarded several literary prizes, including the Before Columbus Foundation American Book Award, the Pen Oakland Josephine Miles Award, and the University of California, Irvine, Chicano/Latino Literary Prize. He has also published several textbooks for teaching Spanish at the high school and college levels: *Tu mundo, Nuestro mundo, Pasaporte al mundo 21,* and *Mundo 21* (Houghton Mifflin, 2000). He did his undergraduate studies at California State University, Long Beach, and his graduate studies at Stanford University. He currently teaches at the University of California, Davis, where he directs the Spanish for Native Speakers Program.

FRANCISCO X. ALARCÓN, poeta y educador chicano, nació en Los Ángeles, California, en 1954, se crió en Guadalajara, México, y ha publicado diez libros de poesía, entre ellos: *Body in Flames / Cuerpo en llamas* (Chronicle Books, 1990), *De amor oscuro / Of Dark Love* (Moving Parts Press, 1991 y 2001), *Snake Poems: An Aztec Invocation* (Chronicle Books, 1992), *No Golden Gate for Us* (Pennywhistle Press, 1993), y *Sonnets to Madness and Other Misfortunes / Sonetos a la locura y otros poemas* (Creative Arts Book Company, 2001). Dos de sus libros de poemas bilingües para niños, *Jitomates risueños y otros poemas de primavera* (Children's Book Press, 1997) y *Del ombligo de la luna y otros poemas de verano* (Children's Book Press, 1999), recibieron el Premio de Honor Pura Belpré de la American Library Association en 1998 y 2000. Ha publicado otros dos libros de poemas bilingües para niños: *Los ángeles andan en bicicleta y otros poemas de otoño* (Children's Book Press, 1999) e *Iguanas en la nieve y otros poemas de invierno* (Children's Book Press, 2001). Ha sido becario de las fundaciones Danforth y Fulbright, y entre otros premios literarios que ha recibido están: el American Book Award de la Before Columbus Foundation, el Pen Oakland Josephine Miles Award, y el Premio Literario Chicano de la Universidad de California, Irvine. También ha publicado varios libros de texto para la enseñanza de español a nivel de escuela secundaria y a nivel universitario: *Tu mundo, Nuestro mundo, Pasaporte al mundo 21,* y *Mundo 21* (Houghton Mifflin, 2000). Hizo sus estudios para la licenciatura en la Universidad Estatal de California en Long Beach y sus estudios de postgrado en la Universidad de Stanford. Actualmente enseña en la Universidad de California, Davis, donde dirige el Programa de Español para Hispanohablantes.

About the Translator

FRANCISCO ARAGÓN translated into English the poems included in the sections "Body in Flames," "Of Dark Love," and "Sonnets to Madness and Other Misfortunes." He is a native of San Francisco and holds degrees in Spanish from the University of California, Berkeley, and New York University, as well as a master's degree in English from the University of California, Davis, where he was awarded an Academy of American Poets Prize in 1999. He is a former editor of the *Berkeley Poetry Review,* and his translations have appeared in *Chelsea, Luna, Nimrod, Poetry Flash,* and *ZYZZYVA.* His own poetry has been published in the anthologies *American Diaspora: Poetry of Displacement* (University of Iowa Press, 2001) and *Inventions of Farewell: A Book of Elegies* (W. W. Norton, 2001). He is the founding editor and publisher of Momotombo Press and is currently a fellow at the University of Notre Dame.

FRANCISCO ARAGÓN tradujo al inglés los poemas de las secciones tituladas "Cuerpo en llamas," "De amor oscuro," y "Sonetos a la locura y otros poemas" de este volumen. Originario de San Francisco, obtuvo una licenciatura en español de la Universidad de California, Berkeley, y de la Universidad de Nueva York, y una maestría en inglés de la Universidad de California, Davis, donde fue galardonado con un premio de la Academia de Poetas Americanos en 1999. Es ex-editor de la revista *Berkeley Poetry Review*. Sus traducciones ha aparecido en varias revistas literarias como *Chelsea, Luna, Nimrod, Poetry Flash,* y *ZYZZYVA*. Poemas de su propia creación ha sido publicados en las antologías *American Diaspora: Poetry of Displacement* (University of Iowa Press, 2001) e *Inventions of Farewell: A Book of Elegies* (W. W. Norton, 2001). Es fundador y editor de la editorial Momotombo Press y actualmente es becario de la Universidad de Notre Dame.